Threads of Resilience

Woven Stories of My Life

Chester Williams

Copyright © 2024 Chester Williams
All rights reserved.

Contents

Chapter 1 - The Train 1
Chapter 2 – Mental Health 6
Chapter 3 – Wee People Club 10
Chapter 4 – Another Brother 14
Chapter 5 – Prejudice Appears 21
Chapter 6 - Swimming 25
Chapter 7 – Fighting and Singing 28
Chapter 8 – Getting a Job 34
Chapter 9 – The Brothel 38
Chapter 10 – The Concert 45
Chapter 11 – Puppy Love 49
Chapter 12 – Jail Time 55
Chapter 13 – A Lost Child 58
Chapter 14 – Meeting my Wife 63
Chapter 15 – Juke Joint 69
Chapter 16 - Churches 74
Chapter 17 – The Sauna 80
Chapter 18 – Upper Peninsula Travels 84
Chapter 19 – The Bahamas 87
Chapter 20 – Bahamas Again 92
Chapter 21 - Sports 98
Chapter 22 – Meeting my Father 102
Chapter 23 – Family Reunions 108
Chapter 24 – My First Son 111
Chapter 25 – An Amazing Trip 116
Chapter 26 – Police Brutality 125
Chapter 27 – A Fall 129
Chapter 28 – Southwest Ho! 136

Chapter 29 – Finding a Family Home 140
Chapter 30 – Snow Birds 144
Chapter 31- Reflections 149

Introduction

Hi,

My name is Chester Williams, and I must confess, I am not a writer. In fact, I have never tackled a lengthy report in my entire life. However, where I truly excel is in the art of conversation and connecting with people. Throughout my life, I have held a true passion for meeting and conversing with people. I do not discriminate; my enthusiasm for conversation knows no bounds.

I give thanks to my mother, who drilled in my head to always be the best I can be and to take care of my siblings. My initial upbringing was not ideal, but by working hard, setting goals, and staying focused, I managed to create a safe and stable life for my family.

When I was young, I always envisioned writing about my life and my family, but living always got in the way. Now that I am older and have the time, I want to share some of my experiences with you, the reader. Now, my life experiences do not include anything fantastic, famous, or mind-altering, but they do display examples of how one can succeed in America. If you find my ramblings even the remotest bit interesting or inspiring, I thank you and appreciate you for taking the time to read my book. Writing this book has been hard, as it took many hours of pondering and head-scratching to get my thoughts on paper. Happily, though, I have completed this task, and I look forward to staying on the right track to maybe even another book!

Sincerely,

Chester –*Threads of Resilience*

Chapter 1-The Train

In the heart of the rural South, in the town of Bessemer, Alabama, my mother's story unfolded against a backdrop of hardship. She was raised by her older sister, as her mother died when the children were very young. There were nine siblings in her family. The struggle for survival took the form of sharecropping, schooling was minimal, and the family struggled to make a life for themselves. They worked tirelessly on a farm bequeathed to them by the benevolent white owner, raising vegetables for sustenance. It was not an easy way to make a living. To make matters worse, they were terrorized by the local Ku Klux Klan, casting a shadow of fear over their already difficult lives. Eventually, they had to leave the farm and seek refuge in a nearby town. The details of their survival are a true testament to resilience in the face of adversity.

The tight-knit family consisted of four girls, five boys, and no parents. The absence of parents cast a heavy responsibility on the oldest sister, who became the main caregiver. In the midst of these challenging family circumstances, my mother met a young man who took interest in her. Unfortunately, he was really interested in taking advantage of a young, naïve girl. Having no parents to run interference or provide any advice, it wasn't too long before my mother was pregnant. She gave birth to a baby boy. Not really knowing much about raising children, and trying to navigate the complexities of parenting, she left him at home while she worked. During one of these workdays, the baby's grandmother saw her walking and asked, "Honey, where is your baby?"

"He's fine… I left him with a bottle in his bed," my mother replied.

"Oh, honey, don't do that. You bring him over here when you working."

This is how my older brother came to be raised down south by his grandmother. I wasn't around then, but I imagine my mother was not ready to be a "mother". She had never really known her own mother, so she had little reference on how to take care of a child. Maybe it was a relief to my mother to have someone else help raise her baby boy. I do remember she didn't talk about him much, so maybe she felt guilty about leaving him with his grandmother.

A few years after, I was born, and then two years later, my younger brother was born. Despite sharing the same father, my mother did not marry him. She often told me she couldn't marry him because he was simply "too mean"! Her choice not to marry my father because of his unkindness reflects her determination to create a safe home for us. Imagining her feelings, I can only assume that she must have experienced isolation and loneliness, navigating life with two young children. Desiring change and recognizing the limited opportunities for young black women in the rural south, my mother sought a better future for us.

Prior to this, her brothers and sisters had all moved north to Ohio, Michigan, Illinois, and Pennsylvania. There were more jobs available in these places, so my mother decided to move to Ohio where her two brothers lived. This decision brought us to a life where I didn't meet my real father until I was much older. But it was a life that did provide more opportunities. I have so often wondered what went through my mother's mind as she made the decision to uproot her life with two young children and go to a place she knew nothing about.

On the day we left, my mother boarded a train in Alabama with my brother—a baby—and me—a toddler. She struggled with us but found a seat in the crowded train. In my mind's eye, I can see my mother overwhelmed, excited for change, and tired. She must have been more than glad to be off her feet. As the train headed north, we all dozed to the lull of the chugging train. People got on and off along various stops. Having to go to the bathroom, my mother asked a kindly looking white lady if she would watch me while she and my baby brother went to the bathroom. "Of course. Take your time," the lady offered.

Upon coming back to her seat, my mother did not see me or the white lady. Thinking she had missed us, she frantically searched the car. "Chester Lee, Chester Lee—where are you?" she hollered. Over and over again, she searched. Finally, she found the conductor and told him what happened.

"Don't worry they have to be on the train. The train has not stopped" He assured her. He quickly went to the other cars, looking for me.

"Chester Lee! Chester Lee!" they both called. In the last car, in a corner, they heard me calling, "Mama! Mama!" There I was, with the kind lady in the dark corner of the very last car. The lady was feeding me candy to keep me quiet. Well, it didn't work. I answered my mother immediately.

The conductor confronted the woman, "Ma'am, what are you doing with that child?"

"I'm helping out that woman," she pointed to my mother.

My mother, in tears, just shook her head.

"I'm afraid you have to come with me", the conductor said. My mother grabbed my hand from the woman. I wasn't sure what had happened, but I was happy to have the candy the lady had given me.

"Chester Lee, come with me and sit down," my mother said with obvious relief.

At the next train station, we witnessed the conductor and police escort the kind-hearted white lady off the train. My mother rose to her feet as the lady passed by, casting a gaze that could pierce through steel. If looks could kill, a tragedy might have unfolded. To this day, I have little memory of the train ride, but I contemplate the potential outcome had the lady's ill intentions succeeded. Life, as it turns out, is remarkably fragile. Chance events can significantly alter the course of one's journey. A thread can be fragile, or a thread can be strong. The threads in my life were just being formed.

Chapter 2 – Mental Health

Arriving in Ohio was a new world for all of us. My mother was astounded at all the available work. She managed to get a job at a factory where the employees built radios and televisions. The pay was much better than down south, but it still was not a lot of money for a family of three. She was happy to be reunited with her two older brothers. They also helped us financially as much as they could. In time, they both became an important part of my upbringing.

We were very poor. Our house did not have an indoor toilet. There was an outhouse in our yard which had to be emptied by the Rotor Rooter truck. It was very scary to use that outhouse, especially at night and in the freezing cold winter. Our front yard did not have grass, cinders only. Mother made us rake the cigarette butts out of the cinders as one of our chores. None of these circumstances bothered me because all the neighbors were in the same boat as us.

Mother started dating again. She did enjoy men! I imagine she wanted to get with someone who could help her with the normal day-to-day costs of living and raising her children. You have to remember that my mother was still a young lady who enjoyed having a good time. My real father's co-worker, Wayne, had moved to Ohio about the same time we did. Mother was happy to see him, and they started spending time together. It wasn't long before my mother was pregnant again. This time, she had a baby girl. Unfortunately, she and Wayne had a falling out, and Mother found herself with three little ones. Life was still a struggle.

Along came Charley. Mother really thought he was the one. They got married, and again, she was in the "family way". As time passed, there were a few incidents that led Mother to question Charley's sanity. He would accuse her of lying and cheating even though all she did was work, play cards, take care of the house, and take care of us. Plus, she was still pregnant!

It wasn't long before his behavior became so stressful that Mother was afraid for our safety. Charley became paranoid and accused Mother of the most ridiculous things. "You are not going to Mrs. Water's house tonight for cards!" he shouted. "She is the devil!"

Mother looked at him and calmly said, "The only devil here is YOU!" And off she went to her weekly card game.

When she arrived back home, the kids were in bed, but where was Charley? "Charley! Charley, are you here?" she shouted. There was no answer. Puzzled, she started searching the small trailer. Charley was nowhere to be found. "I know darn well he did not leave my childen' alone in this house!"

She was terrified and worried at the same time. Charley's behavior had changed so much she had no clue as to where he could be. Bewildered, she plopped down on her bed and stared into space. *Thump, thump, thump* startled her from her reverie. "What is that noise?" She jumped up and followed it.

Walking out of the trailer, she searched around the little structure. Again, she heard the thumping and it sounded like it was coming from underneath the neighbor's house. *How is this possible?* she thought. Bending down, she shouted, "Charley, is that you?" All she heard back was more thumping. Running into the trailer, she found a flashlight and went back out to investigate the noise. She was immediately shocked. There was Charley, hiding under the house. "Charley, get out from under this house, right now!" Charley just lay there, staring into space.

Not knowing what else to do, she called the fire department. "Please don't put on the sirens. I just need to get my husband out from under the house."

Mother was appalled and embarrassed by the spectacle of her husband under the house. Back then, there was not much help for mental health issues, so the firemen were probably the only ones to call. They came and managed to drag Charley out from under the house. They took him to the local hospital where he was placed in a mental health wing for observation.

Well, I guess Charley is not the answer for me, thought Mother. *He is just plain crazy, and I can't deal with that.* The stigma of a mental illness was a definite driving factor in my mother's reaction. It wasn't long after the incident that she left him and got back together with Wayne. After all, they had a baby daughter together. They both agreed to work together and try to make a go of life for themselves and the kids. After she got out of the mess with Charley, Wayne and Mother eventually got married.

This marked the onset of my mother's newfound stability as a married woman. Little did she realize the profound impact her choice of husband would have on my brother and me. Once more, the choices made by the adults in my life carved a path where the threads of my own journey were tested and stretched.

Chapter 3 – Wee People Club

Growing up in a poor, black neighborhood, we really didn't have a lot of structured places to play. We all just ran around the small area, hung out, and played imaginary games. Most of the families living there had little money and many kids. One lady, Mrs. Jackson, was the queen of our neighborhood. She recognized the need for us kids to have some place productive and safe to hang out. She started a club in her home for all of us.

Her home had a large front porch where she would sit and talk with us. Eventually, she added games, books, music, and even a pool table. All of us kids loved going there. Her husband helped her out and decided to form a club, calling it the "Wee People Club". Whenever we had nothing else to do, we would head out and go to the club. Mrs. Jackson seemed to have so much patience with us. She even gave us small snacks and drinks during the day. I remember, sometimes, all of us kids would get rowdy and act up, but Mrs. Jackson had the ability to keep us in line without much effort. She was an amazing lady!

The club became so popular that kids from other neighborhoods started to visit. Their parents would drop them off after getting Mrs. Jackson's approval. She never turned anyone away. But she did have rules. If someone got in trouble or wouldn't behave at the club, they were not allowed to come back for two weeks. This simple rule alleviated many of the kids' bad behavior. Over a few years, word got around about what Mrs. Jackson was doing for our community, and the township in our city took notice.

The commissioners somehow came up with some monetary support and built a small building naming it the "Wee People Club." Mrs. Jackson continued her support of this project by managing the club and keeping the building clean and spotless. Without Mrs. Jackson, the entire project would have floundered and died. I don't think she ever received any compensation for what she accomplished. Mrs. Jackson was one person who saw a need in our neighborhood and managed to create a legacy to benefit the kids.

The club went on for many years until Mrs. Jackson died. Unfortunately, after that, the building sat empty. I had grown up and moved away by then. Whenever I drove by that empty building on visits home, it made me remember all the good times we had in the club.

Another memory from our little neighborhood involves a lady we tormented. She was the exact opposite of Mrs. Jackson. Don't all neighborhoods seem to have a cranky old lady the kids make up stories about? Mrs. Abby was ours. She lived by herself and had no children. And she did not like kids on her property. Her house was on the corner, very close to the road. If kids walked by her house talking loudly and laughing, she would come out and yell "Go home!"

Now, this just caused us kids to torment her all the further. Whenever a group of us were walking by, we would yell "Abbbbyyyyy! Abbbyyyyy!" distorting her name, and then we would take off running and laughing like crazy. She would always come to her door when we did this, screaming at us to go home.

That was not good behavior on our part, but it was very typical of young kids reacting to a grouchy old lady. We never got into trouble for teasing her but only because she never could see who did the yelling. Years later, after she died, for some reason the township tore down her house and built a playground on that corner. Ironically, they named it after Mrs. Abby! So, the few families who still live in the neighborhood can play and have fun in the very area where the crabby old lady lived.

Over the years, the original families in the old neighborhood got better jobs, better opportunities, and moved from Searsville. Still, people did not forget that small community. A few years ago, a reunion of all former residents was organized by some of the older residents. People came together and fellowshipped and reminisced. So far, this has happened annually and has been taken over by the younger people. The streets are blocked off for one day. Food and music are provided for the enjoyment of everyone. Even poor, small communities can provide great experiences for the people living there when everyone contributes what they can, providing a strong safety net for all.

Chapter 4 – Another Brother

After Mother married Wayne, over the next 20 years, they managed to expand our family to include a dozen children! Despite their growing family, we still lived in the same two bedroom house in Searsville. Being one of the older kids, my chores included dumping dirty diapers, raking the front yard, picking up after the younger kids, and helping mother in the kitchen. At the time, as most kids did, I preferred to play around the neighborhood. But the chores did teach me how to take care of myself and others.

One of my chores was to walk to the meat packing house with a bucket. The packing house was a slaughterhouse for pigs and was only about five minutes from our house. My nose still tingles remembering the hot days of summer when the stench of pigs covered the entire area. During the slaughter of the pigs, the facility had a number of trucks waiting to accumulate all the parts not to be sent to market. All the ears, feet, tails, and snouts were thrown down a large chute to be loaded into the waiting trucks. The facility allowed all of us black people to come and take the discarded parts. We had to do this quickly because the meat could spoil or become covered in flies. I was good at climbing up and grabbing as many parts as I could, filling my bucket. Being from the south, most black folks enjoyed eating this type of meat. Where richer white families grazed on steak, my family happily ate thrown away pig parts! My mother was happy to get this free meat to help feed her large family. Eventually, the owner of the facility changed his policy and no longer got rid of those pig parts. Capitalism took over, and all pig parts were sent to market!

Even with Wayne's help and the free pig parts, Mother did not have enough money for all of us. My brother and I often got left out because Wayne took care of his own before us. Oftentimes, my uncles stepped up and helped out my mother financially. I remember a few Christmases where we had to wait for our presents. Because of this, it was at a fairly young age that I realized Santa Claus was but a pipe dream. My uncles had a large part in shaping my family values. They both cared about my brother and me, which provided us a father figure to look up to. I can still hear them telling us how we should conduct ourselves, how we should work, and how we should be respectful to others.

When I was 15 years old, there came a knock on our door. One of my younger sisters peeked out the window and said, "Who's there?"

"I'm your brother. Let me in!" he replied.

My sister went running into mother's room, hollering, "Mama, Mama, there's a man at the door, and he says he's my brother!" Mother jumped up and ran to the door and threw it open. In walked a young man a couple of years older than me. *Who is this?* I wondered.

Mother immediately gathered the young man in her arms. "This is your brother! James, I am so glad you're here," Mother exclaimed with tears in her eyes. She explained how James had been raised down south by his grandmother. Mother had been in touch over the years but never had the ability or money to get James to Ohio. I was astounded. I had an older brother!

James moved in with us and found a job. I really don't remember where we all slept, but we were all very close in the two-bedroom house. Eventually, James got a car. That was the coolest thing, as we only had the old family station wagon. I had a learners permit, so I really shouldn't have been driving by myself. Despite that, I asked, "James, can I borrow your car to go to store?"

James was so easy going he gave me the keys. "Hurry back. I have a date tonight."

"Sure thing," I replied.

After jumping in the car, all thoughts of returning the car left my mind. I drove across town, not to the store, to see a young lady I liked. As I pulled up in the car, Mary came running out. "Nice car. I didn't know you had a car like this. Hey, can we go downtown?" she exclaimed.

"Sure", I answered, not bothering to tell her it wasn't my car.

"You have to go ask my father," Mary said breathlessly. Right away, I was afraid. Her father was a big man who came across as very stern. Getting up my nerve, I ventured into the house.

"Sir, can I take Mary downtown?"

Glaring at me, he replied, "Yes you can, young man, but make sure you get her back at midnight. Not one minute later. Twelve o'clock midnight."

Smiling, I thanked him and ran back outside to tell Mary.

We cruised down the quiet streets of Sandusky, waving at our friends as we passed. A sense of regal satisfaction filled my heart as I noticed Mary's eyes were shining brilliantly and her smile stretched from ear to ear. We circled the streets for awhile until I came up with a great plan.

"Mary" I asked, the excitement palpable in my voice," Do you want to go to the drive-in?"

Her eyes sparkled and a huge smile adorned her lovely face as she eagerly agreed to go. "There's a movie there I've been dying to see forever!"

Heading towards the drive-in, I didn't care what movie was playing; my hopes were set on a different kind of action—in the make-out department! We pulled into the nearly deserted drive-in, and I strategically chose a spot away from the other cars.

Soon enough, we were snuggled up in the front seat, lost in a world of passionate kisses. In my mind, I dared to hope for more, but my hopes were soon crushed when, attempting to explore uncharted territories, I found myself airborne, crashing into the back seat with a bewildered shout.

"What the heck!" I shouted, rubbing my slightly bruised ego.

Wide-eyed, Mary warned, "Don't even try to go there. When I get home, my mother will check my underwear. And I'm not going to pay that price!"

Now, I was not a little person, but Mary was tall for a girl and obviously very strong, as she had easily tossed me into the backseat. Climbing back into the front seat, I looked at Mary and chuckled, "Let's just watch the movie and be friends."

We settled in, sharing a laugh, and as the movie continued, the flickering lights of the screen added warmth to our unexpected drive-in adventure.

Driving away from the movie, and remembering Mary's father's words, I made sure to have Mary home well before the midnight deadline. Upon leaving Mary's house, I guiltily remembered James' words from hours ago, imploring me to hurry back. *Shoot, he's going to be pissed at me*, I thought. As I stealthily crept into the house, James was not there. I was relieved and went to bed.

Unsuccessfully trying to keep my eyes open, I immediately fell into a deep sleep. Suddenly, James shook my shoulder, and I groggily opened my eyes, waiting for his admonishments. Sternly, James held out his hand and said, "Give me the keys." No anger, no threats, nothing. I could not believe it, but that was the kind of person he was.

Contrite, I could not look my brother in the eyes as I mumbled, "Sorry," and handed over his keys.

Reflecting on this incident, my older brother imparted a lesson that resonates with me even today—the art of being gracious in the face of extreme inconsideration. In that exact moment, it wasn't apparent, but looking back,

I realize the invaluable wisdom he displayed to me about family and forgiveness. I had been far from my best self that night. Despite my less than stellar behavior, my brother, James, demonstrated a remarkable level of composure. He refrained from yelling and carrying on. His response left a lasting impression on me.

Despite my wrongdoing, I found comfort in his unexpected kindness. Of course, it wasn't until years later, upon gaining some wisdom, the true weight of his actions struck me. James, who had every reason to feel put out, chose instead to extend a courtesy that I, in all honesty, did not deserve. It is in moments like these that the true measure of character shines through. My brother's ability to rise above my poor behavior and respond with grace taught me not only the importance of family but also the power of forgiveness. This lesson remained etched in my memory, a reminder that kindness, even when undeserved, has the potential to shape, elevate, and strengthen the threads of our relationships.

Chapter 5 – Prejudice Appears

Searsville was considered the black "ghetto" and was my whole world until I became a teenager. White people pretty much stayed out of Searsville—even the police. With this living environment in mind, my first encounter with prejudice didn't happen until my freshman year in high school. I was in my study hall, sitting with my white friends, Tom and Mary. We always sat together. The day it happened, I had gotten to study hall first, and Mary came in and sat across from me. As Mary plopped in her seat, she quietly said, "Hi, Chester. Did you hear about Tom?"

Before I could respond, a teacher came over and demanded that I move to another table. "Why?" I asked, "I sit here every day."

"Because I said to!" he retorted. This made no sense to me.

"No," I responded. He quickly grabbed me around my shirt neck and started to pull me out of my chair.

What the hell, I thought. *Why is this happening to me?* Quick to anger as only a young man can be, I turned around, picked him up, and body slammed him onto the table! I think he was as stunned as I was. My emotions were all over the place, and I knew I had messed up. There were no second chances for poor black boys. He quickly jumped up, red in the face, and stormed out of the room, heading to the principal's office. Mary looked at me with huge eyes, too stunned to say a word. I wanted to cry, but of course, there was no way I would let anyone see me display that kind of emotion. I saw everyone staring and wanted to run away.

The principal told me I was immediately expelled for two weeks. There was no negotiating; they told me to leave. My mother did not have a car, so I had to walk home along the railroad tracks. I was both sad and scared; I knew what I would face at home—my mother's wrath! My dreams of playing basketball on the freshmen team were done.

"Damn, I was going to start." Now. I would be on punishment and would probably not see the outdoors for at least two weeks. It felt like I had a rock in my stomach as I trudged home along the tracks. Surprisingly, my mother was mad at me but didn't say too much. Unlike the parents of today, she did not even contact the principal to discuss the incident.

After two weeks, I returned to the same study hall. Luckily, there was a different teacher. I was relieved. Sitting down by Mary, it felt like nothing had changed. "What did I do to him to make him act like that?"

"Nothing" replied Mary. "He likes me as a girlfriend, but I don't like him. I think he took it out on you!"

"No way," I said.

But I was wrong because it wasn't too long before this teacher was dating another young student. Back then, in our school, they allowed this kind of behavior. It was disturbing to me because of his attitude toward me. He targeted me when I had not done anything inappropriate. He was the improper one, and he was supposed to be a teacher. It was then I realized life is not fair. After being the other young girl's teacher, he ended up marrying her. How crazy is that!

Forty Years Later:
The teacher's wife, who he had married when she was in high school, became my youngest son's second grade teacher. My son loved her because she was soft spoken, patient, and sweet. To this day, he still remembers her with fondness. I was pretty shocked when she became his teacher because I still had bad feelings about her husband. To my surprise, she was one of the better teachers in the elementary school!

Fifty Years Later:
The very same teacher who had terrorized and disrespected me in high school approached me and apologized at the local donut shop. He came up to me

where I was sitting with my buddies and said, "Chester, I like'd to apologize to you, to let you know what I did to you in high school was wrong. I was wrong. I had never been around black people. I grew up in a small town. What happened shouldn't have happened. Please accept my apology."

Wow, I was floored when he said that in front of all the guys. Smiling, I did accept his apology—even if it was fifty years too late. I shook his hand and said, "No problem. Glad you finally realized what you did."

It did make me feel better because it proves people are not bad all the time. Everyone has a story. My story continues to unravel, sometimes making me quite happy and other times leaving me just shaking my head at the ironies of life. The threads of my life just keep on moving in a variety of directions.

Chapter 6 - Swimming

How many black kids like to swim? Not many in my neck of the woods. We did not have access to any type of swimming lessons. As young kids, the only exposure we had was wading in a creek—a far cry from swimming. In high school, the boys and girls had to swim together in gym class. We all had to complete a swimming class that required us to swim two times across the pool. This was in the deep end. Remember, our only exposure to swimming prior to high school was our community creek, which was not deep at all.

Speaking of that creek, I remember plenty of summer days when we would strip off our clothes and jump into that shallow body of water. But that did not require any type of swimming ability. We pretty much just waded in the water and cooled off by wallowing in the shallow creek. In fact, one time, it got us in 'hot water' when the neighborhood girls stole all our clothes, and we had to walk home with bushes wrapped around us for clothes. My mother whooped my butt when I returned home buck naked!

I digress... back to high school swimming. I jumped into the deep end for my test. The coach walked along the edge with a long pole in case I needed assistance. Luckily, despite my uneasiness with this swimming business, I successfully completed the required laps.

After that, I stayed close to the edge and held on as the other students jumped in.

Our school did not have that many black boys. There were probably 8 of us in total. Everyone swam together, so it wasn't segregated. One large black boy, Mike, climbed out of the pool, and to everyone's horror his penis popped out of his Speedo bathing suit!

"Mike," screamed the coach. "Get into the locker room now!" Now, you would think the coach would deal with Mike alone. But instead, he called all of us black boys into the locker room.

"Boys, I want you to go home today and tell your mother and father to provide each of you with a pair of jeans." We all just stared at the coach. Coach continued, "Bring those jeans to our next swimming class, and I will cut them off and you can all wear them for swimming." So, the white boys could wear Speedos, but we had to wear cut off jeans. *How fair is that?* I thought.

As we all exited the locker room, the eyes of the entire class fixed on us. The coach's unequal treatment had left me feeling conspicuous. One black boy's negative incident had become a shared experience for all of us. In the eyes of the coach, our skin color made us the same. Despite my desire to confront the coach, the weight of shame, frustration, and fear of retribution stifled my voice.

As the school year's final swimming class concluded, our once vibrant cut-off jeans bore the effects of chlorine exposure—faded and rotten. The coach remained unwilling to admit his poor choice of swimming attire for all of us black boys. Once again, I found myself confronted with differential treatment solely due to my race. However, I managed to maintain composure this time, refraining from losing my temper and avoiding unnecessary trouble. My reaction marked a step forward in my growth, a glimmer of progress in the face of continual challenges. I was proving that my threads were becoming stronger and stronger, even when stretched to the breaking point. It was just too bad the threads of our jeans were not as resilient!

Chapter 7 – Fighting and Singing

Living with a mess of people in a small, two-bedroom house is, if anything, a challenge. My mother did what she could to make us comfortable, but sometimes, it was just a bit much. To this day, I really need a larger space to call home. It seemed like there was always someone around, so there was literally no privacy in our home. I don't remember being unhappy, but I always yearned for more and better.

Mother and Wayne had a rocky relationship. They did love each other, but that love was broken up by their many arguments. Being one of the older children, I always got in hot water with my stepfather because I would step up to "protect" my mother. Of course, I would not let anyone else threaten or hurt my mother.

The memory of one such fight still brings goose bumps to my arms. I really don't know exactly what they were going at each other about, but my mother was not one to take any lip. Wayne shouted, "You better get over here right now! Give me some more of those beans!" This really set Mother off.

Mother angrily replied, "You better learn yourself some manners and get your own food."

Raising his hand, Wayne tried to hit my mother. Before I could react, Mother grabbed a butcher knife from the kitchen. With a swipe of her hand, she sliced his whole forearm open! I was terrified. There was little blood. Instead, we could see the white inside portion of his arm, open to the bone. After a trip to the hospital, Wayne became a bit more reasonable when it came to his dealings with our mother.

Another time they were fighting, and right away, I jumped in and tried to get Wayne away from Mother. "Stop it," I yelled.

Wayne eyes blazed when he saw me. "You little shit. Get away from me!" he retorted. He turned around and pushed me away, grabbing his shot gun from the closet. Mother screamed. I ran. Fast. Luckily, I was faster than Wayne and his shot gun.

It wasn't long after that incident that I moved out. I went to live with my Uncle Pete and his wife. They had an extra bedroom and were more than willing to help me get on my feet. At first, things went well. My aunt wanted me to take my little cousin with me wherever I went. I didn't mind so much in the beginning. But a five-year-old can really put a crimp in a teenager's style. My aunt was trying to keep me out of trouble by making me take my cousin everywhere. Eventually, I got really tired of being a built-in babysitter and asked my other uncle, Ned (who was single), if I could move into his extra bedroom. Both my uncles were like fathers to me, and so, of course, he agreed.

Moving in with Uncle Ned went smoothly. He was a confirmed bachelor. I used the extra bedroom in his house. Once I got a job, I told him I would help with the monthly expenses. He really didn't press me on that, but I appreciated him taking me in. It made me want to help him out.

I found myself in stable housing, and I began to look around at what I wanted to do. My one love was singing. The music of the 60s was exciting to me. Rock and roll and the funky sounds made my heart quiver! I happened upon an ad for a local band looking for a singer. They were doing auditions, so I decided to call and give it a try.

Now, I have to admit I had no formal singing training. I had never really sang in front of people. I sang with my friends. I sang along with the radio. And I sang when I was alone. When I got to the audition, there were four or five other people trying out. I was nervous. After a bit, they called me in. The band was there.

"How long have you been singing?" the keyboard player asked.

"About two years," I said.

"So, let's jam. Do you know the Stones, Elton John, Stevie Wonder, and Bad Company?"

"Sure," I said with confidence.

The band started playing, and I sang along. They did have the lyrics for me, so that helped. I aced that audition!

The band called me about a week later and asked me to be their lead singer. "Yes! When is our first gig?" I exclaimed.

"Well, we have to practice first. Let's get together on Thursday," the keyboard player stated. When I met them later that week, they gave me their song list. I had a lot to learn, but I was so happy. The song list became my best friend as I studied it and learned all the words.

The group had a previous singer. That person had quit, and now the band consisted of me (black), one white girl, and three white guys. When I went to the practice, many of their parents were there. Everyone was very pleasant and professional. Because I was joining the group, they needed a new name. One of the mothers suggested we name the group Chocolate Cream. "Great name," we agreed.

Chocolate Cream played all over the state of Ohio. We even made it on the Ohio State campus. The enjoyment of singing paid off. It provided some money and certainly gave me the confidence that I really could sing. The more we played, the more we added songs to our repertoire—including not just rock and roll, R&B, and funk but with the addition of country. I felt like a rock star!

One venue that stands out in my mind was a small club in a rural town called Bucyrus. The owner hired us for a weekend. "I'm not sure my customers will like your music, but I do," he said.

On our first night, the club was packed. We started playing some funky music, and the people seemed to be listening and watching, but no one got on the large, lighted dance floor. Another song, and it was the same result. We were not used to people not dancing. After our first set, we went outside to discuss what to play next. Starting our second set, we featured primarily rock and roll. As we blasted out a Stones song, the dance floor filled up! After that, the crowd danced and rocked all night long. They even stayed on the floor for other genres. It was like the crowd just had to get used to us before they loved us.

I stayed with Chocolate Cream for a couple of years. That was a great time for me. I loved the music. I loved the crowds. I loved the songs. Singing with Chocolate Cream exposed me to a world that I could only dream of before. One thing I never got caught up in was the negative parts of a band—drinking and drugging. I still had my main job. I used the band as a means of enjoyment and extra income. Singing is something I can still do, and it makes me happy.

Singing always reminds me of the profound power of music. Music can uplift, inspire, and unite. Whatever note or song I sing requires my determination to achieve a pleasing harmony. This is a testament to the spirit of humanity, weaving its threads of resilience into the fabric of our existence.

Chapter 8 – Getting a Job

As I mentioned previously, I grew up in a large family. My mother had 13 children, and I was second oldest. My mother worked and my stepfather worked, but neither of them had high-paying jobs. We lived in a two bedroom house and were extremely poor. I had not finished high school, so I was desperate to find a job. In the 60s, it was still possible to get a job without a high school diploma.

Luckily, in high school, I had a great counselor. I stayed in touch with him, and even though I was not a student, he was open to helping me. "Mr. Paxon," I said, "I really need to get a job. Is there any way you can help?"

"Certainly, my boy," he replied quickly. "We get contacted by all of the factories in this area."

I smiled and hoped he would follow through on this promise. A day or two later, Mr. Paxon told me a personnel director would contact me from a local factory. Back then, those kinds of jobs were heaven-sent. The weeks dragged by, and I didn't hear back from anyone. I took it upon myself to contact Mr. Paxon.

"Mr. Paxon, I haven't heard anything from the factory job. Is it still available?"

"It's funny you ask—a local factory just called me and said they need someone to start this following Monday!"

"What? That's great! Thank you, Mr. Paxon," I shouted. I had a huge smile on my face. Little did I know how this would change my life.

On Monday, I showed up promptly at 7:00AM, reporting to the guard shack. I didn't know what to expect, but I was ready to give it my all. This job would allow me to help my mother and give me the ability live on my own.

I was hired by General Motors as a laborer. A laborer does just that—labor. I cleaned huge slug tanks, cleaned bathrooms, made sure the aisles and community areas were clean, and kept the parking lots free of snow and debris. The factory was very large—at the time, it was the largest employer in the area. There were many laborers on all three shifts. I was one of many, but I never felt diminished. Working hard, I especially enjoyed the interactions with all the other employees.

A union factory allowed all of us employees to grow and improve ourselves if we were so motivated. Not everyone in the shop took advantage of this benefit. During my first 15 years working, I witnessed some people who abused the union. I also witnessed people who worked and managed to advance their position in life.

Sometime after my 15th year of work, the factory and the union started doing joint ventures to improve the quality of the product and also improve the working conditions for the employees. The labor pool was targeted. Electricians, plumbers, tool and die, and laborers were all encouraged to apply for a brand new position. The position would be titled Labor Leader. The person would effectively direct a large group of workers. Seniority would not be used to pick the new leaders. The union and factory would decide based on work history and ability to lead. The person applying had to write a resume and cover letter stating why they deserved the new job.

I immediately started thinking about applying for this new position. *There is no way I have a chance*, I thought. *There are people here with college degrees, and I don't even have my high school diploma. But I do have many years of experience and my ability to talk to just about anyone—from the president of the company to a new-hire employee.*

Working with my then girlfriend, now wife, we pounded out a letter highlighting all my good qualities for the new position. I had an advantage of working all over the factory and getting to know a variety of people. Keeping my fingers crossed, I submitted the letter, along with any other required documents, to personnel.

Never thinking I would get the position, six months went by. During my usual work shift, my foreman came up to me. "Chet, come on and follow me."

Intrigued, I followed him. After a few minutes, he said, "You got the new position!"

I was astounded and shouted, "No way!"

"You are going to be the new Labor Leader for all the laborers and janitors. Congratulations!" He showed me where my new office would be built. I felt like I was in a dream—me with an office!

Of course, some of the other employees were angry or jealous about me getting the job. But that didn't last because most of them congratulated me. But truly, even I didn't think I would get it. I may be old-fashioned, but I always believed that hard work pays off. Do the right thing, put up with whatever is thrown at you, and stay true to what you believe in. Because of these beliefs, God was good to me. The blessings were reciprocated because of my work ethic and social behavior. Be nice to people, work hard, and good things can happen.

Chapter 9 – The Brothel

During my older teenage years, I had a group of friends, mostly white, I used to run around with. We never did anything criminal, but we certainly pushed the boundaries. I never drank or did drugs, but I still liked to hang out, talk to girls, and party with everyone. It seemed like we were always on the go—even if we were just hanging out downtown. Some of the experiences we had may not have been morally healthy, but at the time, we certainly enjoyed them!

One day, my friend, Jeff, suggested, "Let's go downtown and see what's going on tonight." I was pretty bored, so I agreed. Jeff had a car, and I jumped in. We picked up a couple of other guys along the way. When we pulled up to the main street downtown, some of our other friends were there. We were all joking and shooting the shit when Jeff said, "Hey, I have an idea. Remember that whore house we went to a couple of months ago… let's go again. I have the cash, so don't worry about paying!" Now I had not been with them when they had gone two months prior. So I was up for it but still a little hesitant, not knowing what to expect.

We all got into Jeff's car and headed for the whore house. It was only about 20 minutes from downtown, so we arrived in no time. There were about four or five other cars in the parking lot. Eagerly, we piled out of the car and walked up to the door. We all tried to look mature as we rang the doorbell, even though none of us were over the age of 18. A blonde-haired lady looked out the peep hole and shouted, "Hold on one minute." We stood there, shuffling our feet for what seemed like a long time. It was more like 10 minutes. Finally, the lady slowly opened the door and said, "Come on in."

We all filed in. There was a large foyer with chairs in it. "Sit down," she instructed. We all sat in the chairs and watched as she sauntered into the adjourning room. Wide-eyed, I looked around and was amazed. It looked like a normal house. I expected something more grandiose for a whore house!

Again, Jeff reminded me not to worry about paying, as it was his treat. I smiled at this. Finally, after we sat and fidgeted and waited for about 20 minutes, six young ladies came out. They all looked very nice and normal—just like any young lady you would see walking around our town! A tall, voluptuous, dark-haired young lady walked up to me, looked me in the eye, and said, "We don't serve your kind here. You have to go." I was confounded and embarrassed. I started to rise out of the chair to leave.

Immediately, Jeff jumped up and said, "Hey we're all here together. It's all or none of us." She replied, "Honey, I'm sorry, but we just don't serve his kind. You all need to leave."

Jeff looked at all of us and said, "Let's get out of here. They don't want our money. It's their loss, not ours." The lady just shrugged her shoulders, turned and walked into the other room. We all filed out the front door.

"Hey, I'm sorry, guys… I didn't want to mess this up for all of you."

"Don't worry. We don't want to waste our money on the likes of those women," all my friends agreed.

As we got back to the car, Jeff said, "Hey I know another house, but it's about 30 minutes from here. How about giving that one a try? It would still be my treat." I was hesitant, thinking the same thing would happen. It is not a good feeling to be singled out and treated less than others—especially by a whore house! Everyone else wanted to go, so I went along, hoping it would be a better experience.

Arriving at the house, it was dark and smaller than the previous house. I looked at it apprehensively, thinking about my prior experience and hoping this would not be a repeat. We all walked up to the house and were immediately admitted. Right away, there were five or six girls staring at us. They were all pretty. I was anxious about being treated as a second-class citizen who couldn't even be serviced by a white whore. None of them said a word to any of us. This was a relief to me.

One of the girls came up to us and whispered, "Hey, guys, you can each pick one of us. You get five minutes." Well, none of us were thinking about the five minutes—we were just happy not to get rejected again. But five minutes? That is not long enough for a dog! So, one young lady led me into a room and started to fondle me. Before I knew it, she said, "Time's up. I need more money if you want to stay longer."

I was startled and said, "No way, I'm not paying."

I left the room and went out to the main area and sat down. *What a rip off*, I thought. It wasn't a minute or two later when all the other guys came out looking just like I did—disgusted and dejected. One of the ladies came out and said, "Thanks, Guys. Come back soon." None of us replied. We did not have a good time, and it was a complete waste of money.

Returning to the car, one of the windows on the side of the car was busted out. "Son of a bitch, now they messed up my car!" Jeff shouted. There was money taken from the glove box, too.

What a shit show, I thought. I looked at Jeff and said, "This is the last time I ever do anything like this."

"Hey, you shouldn't feel that way. I took the bill. Don't worry about it, okay?" Jeff replied. That was the difference between Jeff and I—he had money to waste, and I would have been devastated to lose that much.

Returning home, Jeff dropped us off and said "Hey I'll see you all on Saturday. We'll go to the quarry and skinny dip."

I looked at Jeff and said, "I'm up for that, but I'm not getting naked in front of everyone!" They all laughed at me. I didn't care. No way was I skinny dipping. Plus, I did not know how to swim all that well.

On Saturday, we met up downtown, and everyone got in my car. We drove to the quarry and parked. I still couldn't believe I would see naked people (girls and guys) swimming in the broad daylight. We got to the swimming area, and sure enough, there were probably 20 to 30 girls and guys jumping off rocks, stark naked. Of course, I was the only black person in the whole area. Before I knew it, Jeff had stripped and was climbing on a rock to jump in the water. Hollering, he tucked his feet in and did a bombshell dive into the water! I could not believe what I was seeing. Mesmerized, I quietly sat down and watched until it was time to go.

"Man, you don't know what you missed. The water felt so cool and refreshing," exclaimed Jeff.

"I told you I wasn't skinny dipping," I stated bluntly.

"Your loss man," replied Jeff.

"But Jeff, if the cops come, couldn't you get in trouble for skinny dipping?" I inquired.

"Well sure, but they don't usually come to the quarry," he replied. With that, we left to go back home.

The next day I was telling my black friends about what I had seen at the quarry. "There were naked girls and guys swimming in broad daylight."

"No way. You're lying" they said.

"Come on, I'll take you there, and you can see for yourselves!" I took three of my black friends out to the quarry. We walked in, and to my horror, there was no one there. No one was even swimming!

My friends looked at me, "You lying heifer. We knew you made this one up."

I stuttered, "No, there were people here the other day. I wouldn't make up anything like that." Well they didn't believe me and called me names I can't repeat here.

I called Jeff when I got home and told him what happened. He started laughing, "Chester, people only swim there on Saturdays. Next time, check with me when you want to show your friends naked swimmers!" I hung up and just shook my head. To this day, I have never seen anything like the spectacle I saw at the quarry. And I never went back to either the quarry or a whore house!

Chapter 10 – The Concert

Three of my friends were dating young ladies attending Purdue University. Coincidentally, The Temptations were scheduled to perform there. One day, my friend asked, "Hey, Chester, would you like to go with me and a few other guys to see The Temptations this weekend? My girlfriend can get tickets, and I'm planning on driving."

Having never been to a formal concert, I was intrigued. "That sounds great. I don't have anything going on this weekend with the band."

My mother had always been a huge fan of The Temptations. Whenever their songs played on the radio, she would stop what she was doing, turn up the volume, and tell us kids to hush. She once mentioned that one of the members was her cousin. Armed with this information, I was particularly excited to see The Temptations perform live.

Setting out early on Friday morning, the guys were all excited and looking forward to the concert. The six-hour drive to Purdue was underway, and about half-way there, my friends decided to kick off the festivities. Beers were cracked open, joints were lit, and the atmosphere took a celebratory turn—except for me. I was not happy about this situation at all. Not only did I abstain from drinking or doing drugs, but I did not want to be driving in a car with a group of guys under the influence.

Quickly speaking up, I asserted, "Hey guys, you need to hold off on all this until we get to Purdue."

They all looked at me and countered, "What, we're just having a little drink before we get there. Nothing's going to happen!"

Standing firm on my beliefs, I stated, "Either you stop, or you can let me out at the next stop, and I'll find my own way home." Faced with this ultimatum, they all agreed to wait and, reluctantly, put down the beers and joints. Despite this, I still was feeling very uncomfortable because they had already consumed enough to be affected. I insisted, "Let me drive. I'm the only one who is 100% sober. I can get us there in one piece!"

After I took control of the wheel, we arrived safely in Purdue. Excitedly, we contacted the girlfriends and found out, to our dismay, we could not stay at their place. Of course, because of the concert, finding available hotel rooms proved challenging. After an extensive search, we finally found a hotel with a couple of available rooms. Settling in for the night, we eagerly anticipated the concert scheduled for the next day.

Arriving at the concert, we were met with a massive crowd, predominantly composed of enthusiastic young girls. It was evident The Temptations had a magnetic effect on the female audience. Upon finding our seats, we were all dismayed at how far back from the stage we were. As the concert started, the people in front of us promptly stood on their feet and remained standing for the rest of the show. I had to navigate to the aisle to catch a clear view the band! Despite the poor seating arrangement, I thoroughly enjoyed the performance, and the show was nothing short of amazing.

Following the concert, some of the guys accompanied their girlfriends. The rest of us returned to the hotel. One of the guys took the initiative to invite some girls over, creating a lively atmosphere with music and drinks. Unfortunately, none of the young ladies appealed to me, so I quietly left the room.

The evening air was warm, making it pleasant to stroll around the campus. Eventually, I stumbled upon a charming little café and decided to get a bite to eat. To my delight, the café featured a live band playing bluegrass music. The band even extended an invitation for anyone to join them on stage. While I found this idea intriguing, I refrained from participating since I wasn't familiar with any of their music. Instead, I sat back, relaxed, ate the food, and enjoyed the show put on by the band. Before I realized it, the show was over, and the café was closing for the night.

Returning to the hotel room, I opened the door only to be met with a scene of bodies strewn all over the beds. It seemed like everyone had indulged a bit too much and passed out wherever they were sitting. I quietly made my way around the room, used the bathroom, and concluded that I might get better sleep in the car. So, that's exactly where I headed for the night.

The next morning, as we were leaving, the guys told me I had apparently missed out on an entertaining night. I simply smiled and chose to say nothing. The journey back was more subdued than our trip there. All of the guys were nursing hangovers (except for me). Arriving back in Sandusky, I stopped to see my mother. Her eyes lit up as I shared the story of seeing her cousin perform at the concert. Reflecting on the experience, I couldn't help but think that my first concert experience would have been even more memorable if my mother could have been there with me.

Chapter 11 – Puppy Love

I met many young ladies at the Wee People Club and at the skating rinks. One that caught my eye at the skating rink was a girl called Deb. She could really skate well. There were many guys who wanted to be with her, but she didn't give them the time of day. Guess what? She liked me. One day, she looked at me with her big brown eyes and said, "Chester, come on and skate with me." My heart was beating hard as I took her hand. I thought I was in love (of course, it was probably more like lust)!

After that night, we talked on the phone for hours. We made all kinds of plans on what we were going to do once we became old enough. We talked and we laughed. I was head over heels about Deb. Unfortunately her mother was very strict with her. She would not let Deb on a date with me. That made both of us very frustrated and sad.

One Saturday, Deb called me and excitedly said, "Hey, you can come over!"

"What do you mean?" I asked.

"My mother had to go in to work. Somebody called in sick, so she had to cover. You can come right now. But you have to come around to the back door."

"Okay. I'll be there in about 10 minutes," I said as I hurriedly got dressed and rushed out the door.

I practically ran all the way to her house. Breathing fast, I went to the back door and lightly knocked. Deb opened the door and pulled me in. She only had a robe on, and I immediately got excited seeing her dressed so skimpily. Deb grabbed my face and kissed me. Even though I liked that immensely, I pulled back because I was worried her mother would return. "Hey," I said, 'Let's go into the other room where we can be more comfortable."

We went into the living room and pulled some big pillows on the floor. We lay down and started making out. Now, I was in heaven. After about 20 minutes, I heard a noise. "Is that the garage door opening?" I asked Deb.

She quickly jumped up and whispered, "Get your clothes and get out the back door—fast!" I moved so fast you would have thought I had superpowers. I was half dressed as I ran into some bushes in the back yard to finish putting my clothes on.

I managed to get home in no time. I was so scared.

About two hours later, I heard mother talking to someone in the kitchen. "Chester, come here," called mother. I walked out, and the first person I saw was Deb, and she was crying! I got so scared and nervous. *What the heck is going on?* I thought. Both my mother and Deb's mother glared at me. I swallowed nervously. Deb's mother sternly said, "You are not welcome at my house ever again. If I see you around my daughter, I will call the police!"

All I could say was, "Yes, ma'am."

She grabbed Debs' hand and stormed out of the house. Mother glared at me. "Chester, you stay away from that girl."

Again, all I could say was, "Yes, ma'am." I didn't get in any trouble from my mother, but I could not have any contact with Deb. That made me sad.

For the next three weeks, Deb did not show up at the skating rink. Her girlfriends were there, and I asked, "Have you seen Deb?"

"Yeah, we saw her, but she's in the doghouse because of you! She has been grounded, so you won't see her around here."

Dumbly, I replied, "Why? I didn't do anything."

They all just stared at me. The next week, Deb did show up at the rink. She came over to me and said, "I really can't talk to you. My mom is in the parking lot watching." She glanced over her shoulder to the glass door. Finally, her mom left, and we could talk.

"Deb," I said, "I'm sorry if you got in trouble. But how did your mom know anything? I ran away, and she didn't see me."

"She came in and immediately sensed something was up. And then she saw something on the rug where we were laying. My mom is so mad at me. She is taking me to Detroit to live with my aunt." Deb had tears in her eyes when she told me. "She thinks I'm going to get pregnant if I stay here."

"Oh, Deb, is there anything I can do?"

"I'm afraid not. We are leaving next week."

Sadly, that was the end of my relationship with Deb. Who knows if we would have even stayed together? We never got the chance to try. The whole experience left me with a bad taste in my mouth.

Six or more years went by, and of course, Deb was only a girl in my past. My mother was not feeling well, and her doctor admitted her to the hospital for tests. We were all concerned as she had been feeling poorly for awhile. She was in the hospital for about a week before the doctors determined she had diabetes. They put her on insulin. I still remember how they trained her to inject herself using an orange.

While mother was in the hospital, she had shared a room with Deb's mom. Mother told me, "Chester, Mrs. Haney asked about you when we were sharing the hospital room. She wanted to know how you were doing."

I didn't say much, but it made me wonder why she was asking about me. After all, she had acted like I was the plague when Deb and I were together.

Not long after that, I ran into one of Deb's old friends. She came up to me and said, "Hi, Chester, how are you doing?"

"Okay" I replied. "Have you kept in touch with Deb?"

"Oh yeah, she is still in Detroit. She has three kids. She met a guy there not long after she moved there and ended up getting pregnant. They eventually moved in together, but he went to prison."
I was speechless at this news.

Deb's mom died, and I heard that Deb was back in town for the funeral. Of course, I was curious to see Deb, so I went by her mom's house. I knocked on the door, and it was opened by a woman I really didn't recognize. "Hi" I said. "Is Deb here?"

She smiled and said, "Chester, it's me!"

I was stunned and embarrassed because I had not recognized her. She invited me in, and we sat down to talk. She told me all about her life in Detroit, and she introduced me to her three children. All I could think about was how dramatically changed she was. The Deb I had known was completely different. Life must have thrown some hard knocks at her. After we talked for a while, she had to take a phone call, so I excused myself and left.

I never saw Deb after that. It made me sad to think her mom sent her away to protect her from me. Thinking about how much fun we had back when we were young brought tears to my eyes. The results of her mom's decision had dramatically changed the course of Deb's life. I only hope she is happy and doing well with her children in Detroit.

Chapter 12 – Jail Time

I worked at General Motors for a year or two before they went on strike. During my employment, child support for my son, Link, was automatically deducted from my paycheck and sent to the court. At the time, my hourly pay was not substantial, and I was paying $35 a week.

Unfortunately, when the strike occurred, none of us received any pay. Consequently, the child support payments couldn't be made during the period of the strike. When this situation happened, I immediately called the court to let them know my child support would not be sent until the strike was settled. Sadly, the court would not relent. Instead, they insisted that I send my strike pay (which was $35) to cover the child support.

This presented a significant challenge to me, as I needed that money to meet my basic needs, including being able to eat. The situation placed me in a difficult position, torn between fulfilling my financial obligations to my son and ensuring my own well-being during the strike.

In order to receive our strike pay, we had to walk the picket line. I showed up for my shift on the picket line. It was set up in the entrance to the parking lot for the factory. We all took turns carrying the signs and walking along the parking lot. I had been in the line for a couple of hours when the sheriff pulled up to the plant entrance. The sheriff got out and went up to the line foreman. He announced, loudly, he was here with a warrant to pick me up. Everyone stopped walking, turned, and stared at me. I couldn't believe it and said, "What did I do?"

He replied, "You did not pay your child support." What could I say? He led me into the back seat of the police car. This was my first time ever being arrested, and I was so ashamed.

They drove me over 60 miles to the jail in the county where my son lived. Now, that seemed like an extreme waste of money for my small child support payment! I spent the night in jail and went in front of the judge the next afternoon. The judge ordered me to pay three weeks of child support, which was $105 dollars. I told him I did not have that much money and the plant was on strike. I asked if he could give me a break until the strike ended. He did not relent.

They took me back to jail. I did get a chance to make a phone call. The only person I could call was my Uncle Pete. He drove all the way over to the jail and paid my child support. I told him I would pay him back once the strike ended. He saved my life! I felt so helpless in front of the judge. Almost everyone in that area was white, and I felt completely discriminated against by the judge.

After I got back to Sandusky, I went and talked to the union president and explained to him what had happened. He told me not to worry. I was reassigned to the picket line. My next time walking the picket line was uneventful, and none of my coworkers asked me about why the sheriff arrested me. Thank God for that. Eventually, the strike was settled, and we got back to work. After a few weeks, I caught up on my child support and repaid my Uncle Pete.

The court put so much pressure on me. Yet, the sad part of this situation, unbeknown to me, was my son was not even getting the support I sent. When Link's mother had lost custody, he had moved in with his grandmother, and the support I was sending was going to his mother. This made no sense. Eventually, this situation would be rectified but not until I was in a position to make a difference in my son's life. To this day, whenever I think about this situation, I feel extremely guilty and sad. A child, my son, deserved to be raised better by the adults in his life.

Chapter 13 – A Lost Child

Having an amusement park like Cedar Point in our small town brought many more people to this area. For a young man, this was a great benefit for not only meeting girls but for having a fun place to go. One summer, I met a young lady by the name of Nina—she was a college student working at Cedar Point. We started dating, and I eventually took her to meet my family. Nina was white, but she fit right in with all of my people. They all loved her, and the feeling was mutual. Nina told me her family would not be as accepting of me. Despite this, our connection seemed genuine, and we continued our love story.

As with many love stories, Nina and I found ourselves faced with an unexpected twist in our journey, as she discovered she was pregnant. While we were deeply connected, we shared a mutual understanding we were not ready for the responsibilities of marriage or parenthood. Nina wanted to return to college but felt unable to due to the pregnancy. Feeling trapped, Nina asked my mother, "Mama, would you help me raise this baby?"

My mother, having 13 of her own, replied, "No, honey. You and Chester have to do that."

As soon as Nina heard this, her attitude toward me changed. She said to me, "What am I going do?" Not sure what to say, I said nothing. Maybe I should have been more supportive, but at the time, I was not in any place to give Nina much advice. Later that day, she called her sister. I overheard the conversation. When she told her sister she was pregnant, her sister told her not to come home and to keep that N***** baby away. Nina burst into tears and ran out of the house.

Again, I was paralyzed, not knowing what to do. We were not ready to support and raise a baby. Not long after this, Nina disappeared. No one knew where she went. She called me about a week later and told me she had moved to Columbus. I asked her what she was going to do, and all she would say was for me not to worry about her. A couple of months went by, and I received another call. It was Nina. She said, "I gave the baby away. Don't worry about me or the baby. Bye." She hung up before I could get a word in.

There was nothing to be done. This child of mine was lost to me. I hoped he or she was given to a good, stable family. My life continued on, and the baby became only a memory to me. The whole experience left me feeling responsible, sad, and frustrated. Four years later, when I met a girl, who would become my wife, I even told her about Nina. Little did I know at that time what would happen later on in my life.

Another phone call came thirty years later. "Hello," a voice over the phone line said. "Is this Chester?"

"Yes. Who's calling?" I responded.

"My name is Rita. I adopted your baby son, and I got your number from Nina. Your son's name is Brody, and I was hoping you could come and meet with me."

I was almost speechless, but I managed to agree to come. She proceeded to tell me that Brody had gotten into trouble and had been sent to prison. She wanted to know if I would be interested in going to visit him.

Embarking on a journey to connect with Brody's adopted mother, my wife and I undertook a two-hour drive to her residence, uncertain of the revelations that awaited us. Upon meeting her, she was quite gracious and opened up about her life. She shared precious pictures of Brody's childhood, offering us a glimpse into the formative years I had missed. Meeting Brody's sister added another layer to the narrative. Rita explained that she and Brody's adopted father were divorced. Brody had lived with him during his high school years. The post-high school period marked a challenging phase for Brody, where he encountered difficulties and made poor choices that led him into trouble. The whole experience was surreal, unraveling a trove of information about a baby I had considered lost. My perception of Brody was reshaped from one of complete darkness to understanding. I was happy to visit Brody, even in prison.

Upon reaching the prison, I underwent the necessary security procedures before being led to a room where I came face-to-face with Brody for the first time. It surprised me he bore a resemblance to my eldest son from my marriage with my wife. As he spoke quietly, recounting the chapters of his life, I found comfort in the revelation that his childhood had been stable and happy. In an attempt to share my perspective without making excuses, I explained what had happened when he was born. Brody attentively listened, and to my surprise, he added, "I have a son. He's in Detroit with his mother." The earnestness in his tone conveyed a desire to be actively involved in his son's life and upbringing. The visit was remarkable and gave me hope for Brody's future.

Remarkably, a month later, Nina called me, initiating a conversation that broke a silence of many years. Initially, our exchange was somewhat awkward, given the passage of time. Nina had also been in contact with Brody and secured his permission for her to facilitate a meeting with his son, my grandson. With my wife's agreement, we arranged a weekend visit to Sandusky. The gathering was a success, with everyone enjoying the time together. Although my grandson was a bit reserved, his manners shone through. Following the weekend, Nina invited us to visit Columbus and meet her husband—a Japanese man—and their son.

After more than 30 plus years, Nina and I rekindled our connection. Our son, Brody, set to be released from prison, expressed a strong desire to build a good life. He was determined to be an active part of his own son's upbringing. The events that unfolded taught me a valuable lesson: to hold onto hope and exercise patience, as even after decades, positive and transformative moments can emerge from the most unexpected places.

Chapter 14 – Meeting my Wife

Sandusky is a small town, but the population increases dramatically in the summer because of Cedar Point tourists. During the summer, in the 60s, we used to drive downtown (which was a square) and "buzz" the avenue. This would go on for hours. Everyone would have their cars shining. Muscle cars abounded, and we all wanted to drive the fastest and best-looking vehicle. Most parents never worried about their kids because buzzing the avenue was a safe event. It was a great place for us to meet our friends and hook up with girls!

Our group of friends consisted of both black and white guys. Sandusky didn't really have many race-related problems as compared to larger cities. We had one incident, though, that stands out in my mind. All of us guys were hanging out, and one white dude from out of town started mouthing off. He shouted some scandalous racial remarks, which I won't bother to repeat in this book. Of course, all of us black guys were more than irritated. My white friends also told him to shut up. One thing led to another, and before you could blink, pushing and shoving occurred. My white friend, Mike, and I jumped up and shouted in unison, "Stop! Stop before the police come! We'll get banned from buzzin you a-holes!"

Everyone came to a stop and stared at us. They immediately got back into their cars and went back to what they were doing prior to the fight. I looked at Mike, and he looked at me. I smiled, we high fived, and said, "Hey, we just broke up a race riot!"

There was a Big Boy restaurant right on the corner of the square. This was a local hang-out for young people. The restaurant even had waitresses with skates on who would take your order from the drive up. I did not live far from downtown, and I would eat at the Big Boy quite often. I was considered a "regular" by the staff. The food was typical American cuisine—burgers, fries, hammy subs, spaghetti, and a great ice cream fudge cake. It was 1975, and I was at the counter eating my usual Buddie Boy sandwich and fries. We had buzzed the avenue earlier, but now I was focused on filling my stomach.

One of the waitresses, Beth, had just started work there and was new to the area. She was always nice to me and, today, told me her car had broken down. I enjoyed talking to her, and it certainly didn't hurt that she was cute! "Can you give me a ride to my apartment in Huron after my shift?" she asked me. Even though it would be after midnight, I quickly considered and answered that I would be there after her shift. Not long after midnight, I pulled up to the Big Boy, and out came Beth. She jumped into the front seat saying, "Thanks I really appreciate this."

On the way to her apartment, I mentioned I was in a band. "Would you like to come hear us practice sometime?"

Beth's eyes lit up. "That would be cool" she replied. "Maybe my two girlfriends would like to come with me."

She had moved here from a nearby state and was living with her friends she had grown up with. After I dropped her off, we made a future date so she could come listen to my band practice. She did come and listen to my band. Little did I know this would lead to a life-long relationship with her. We dated for about a month before I kissed her. Within a few years, we moved in together.

I think she told her family (who were all white people) about me as soon as we met. My family accepted her with no questions, and I think she wanted to make her family aware of me because of the way we felt about each other. We had many of the same interests and beliefs—those being music, having a good time, working toward goals, and traveling. We had been raised in very different cultures, but we seemed to agree on things that were important to us.

After about seven months of dating, we planned on driving up to her hometown of Marquette, MI, so I could meet her family. Now, I had never traveled anywhere except down south with my family. Beth told me about her hometown and said the minority there were Native Americans. There were no black people living there! I was a little bit nervous about not only meeting her family but going up to an area with no black people. Don't get me wrong, I have been around white people my whole life, but it was the fact there would be no black folks around for hundreds of miles!

We headed north for her hometown early one summer morning. It was an eight-hour drive straight north until we crossed the Mackinac Bridge. I held my breath going across that five-mile suspension bridge. Once across, we had over two hours to drive toward her hometown. It was a long drive, to say the least. And the last two hours, the scenery was nothing but trees, trees, and more trees! Finally, we made it to Marquette. As I pulled into the driveway, I looked at the large beige house with the wraparound porch and said, "Beth, go ahead and go in. I will wait here. I'm going to rest for a while, and then I'm going to drive to Sault Saint Marie, Canada."

Beth jumped out of the car. I could tell she was excited and anxious to see her family. It had been almost a year since she had been back home. It didn't seem like much time passed before out the door came her mother, Flo.

"Chester, come on in the house. You can't just sit in the car after that long drive!" exclaimed Flo. I stared at her, speechless, and clambered from the car. What else could I do but follow this little lady into her house? "Thanks for bringing Beth home," said Flo. I stuttered, "You're welcome," feeling a bit nervous.

A couple of Beth's sisters were there, and they welcomed me with open arms. They literally hugged me! After a bit of chit chat, Flo stated, "Chester, you can't go to Canada by yourself after that long drive. Bring your luggage in, and you are welcome to stay here."

Smiling, I went and got the luggage out of the car. "Go on upstairs, and your room is the first one on the right." I found the room and tentatively entered. Setting my suitcase down, the first thing I saw was a gun mounted on the wall. *Oh shit*, I thought. Again, I had qualms about staying, but I pushed my feelings down and went on downstairs.

Beth's father, Howard, was in the kitchen. He proceeded to talk to me and said, "Let's head out. I want to show you around this town." We drove in his truck, and he showed me various places. Some of the highlights were the huge Catholic church where he was a head usher, the lake and beach, his Knights of Columbus club, and the quaint downtown area. All the while, he quietly asked me questions and told me about himself. I felt a little more comfortable. On the way back, he said, "When we get home, I'm going to make us a steak on the grill." He grilled both of us a really good steak. This whole experience made me feel like a king, so welcome and accepted by Beth's family.

Unbeknownst to me before we traveled to Beth's hometown, her father had called her (he had been drinking) and told her not to bring me there. Of course, this upset Beth tremendously. Her mother and sisters, more or less, jumped all over her father for saying such an unchristian thing. Her father was a pretty laid back and quiet man, and if he hadn't been drinking, he would have never said anything like that. Of course, his actions once I got there were just the opposite of that phone call. After we left, Beth told me about the prior phone call. It's a good thing I was unaware because I probably wouldn't have gone into the house when Flo invited me! Sometimes, ignorance is better because if I would have left, I would have missed out on a really good experience.

Chapter 15 – Juke Joint

When I first met Beth, I had invited her to come and listen to my band practice. The band practiced at my Uncle Pete's building. He had an after-hours club in Searsville. It was a small building only used for after-hours parties—much like the juke joint made famous in the movie "The Color Purple". It was perfect for band practice because the loud music would not disturb any of the neighbors. Most of the buildings around the after-hours club were empty, so there were no neighbors to disturb.

The first band I was in was called Chocolate Cream. I told you about that group in a previous chapter. Unfortunately, that group had broken up, as local bands often do. I had pulled this new group together and managed all our gigs. Managing the gigs consisted of finding work sites and negotiating payments. My gift of gab and the fact I knew so many people in the area made me pretty good at doing that kind of thing. This new band was made up of three black guys and two white guys. We played mostly R&B and Funk. The name of this group was Funky United Nations (FUN). We had been together for awhile and played around bars in the local area.

Surprisingly, Beth and I liked the same type of music. Knowing she grew up in a rural white community, I assumed she would prefer country music. That was not the case. We made it a date and went to my uncle's after-hours club. The band was there, and we practiced for a couple of hours. The band all met Beth, and they were not inhibited by her being there. In fact, the practice went quite well except for some disagreements on what songs to play. This is normal band dysfunction. Beth did not seem to be bothered by the guys disagreeing and seemed to enjoy listening to the songs we did play. That made me smile.

Later on, for another date, I brought Beth to the after-hours club when it was open and in full-swing. This was quite late after all the other bars in the area were closed, meaning it was the wee hours of the morning! The club was packed full of, mostly, black people dancing, drinking, and eating. Wide-eyed, Beth stayed close to me as we pushed our way through the rowdy crowd. We went into the kitchen, and I introduced her to my Uncle Pete. Smiling at her, with a twinkle in his eye, my uncle said, "Welcome to my club. My nephew better take care of you!"

Beth smiled back and shyly said, "Oh, he has so far. Thanks." I could tell my uncle approved of Beth. We didn't stay long because it was just too crowded.

People from all over came to the club, and the police pretty much stayed away from Searsville. Most of the time, nothing violent happened. It was usually people drinking, dancing, eating, and partying. The guys tried to be like pimps—dressing fancy and walking with a slight hitch. They were mostly concerned about getting with the women. If there was any kind of disturbance, it was usually because of jealousy or couples disagreeing. I do remember one incident of that very sort between two young women.

The club was crammed as usual. The two women strutted in together. "Hey let's get on this dance floor!" they both shouted.

"My boo is here," Willie said as she ran towards him. "What you talkin about girl? He's mine!" retorted Sherry. The tension was palatable. The young man they were arguing about just stood there, wide-eyed. In the blink of an eye, Sherry whipped a knife out of her purse and ran at Willie. It was like a Zorro movie as she carved a W into Willie's cheek. Blood poured down Willie's cheeks as she shrieked like a banshee. All hell broke out as the two girls struggled and screamed. The rest of the crowd began to run out of the club, some not knowing what had happened, others just running away from the noise and violence.

That was an unusual incident. Most nights at the club were pretty low-key with no hints of any kind of violence. My Uncle always told me to stay away from drinking and taking drugs, and that is one of the reasons

I never took part in anything like that. Even when I would go out to the clubs and bars, I stayed sober. Thinking back to those days, I still hear my uncle's voice telling me to stay away from all that kind of stuff.

Uncle Pete always said, 'Boy, don't be letting your friends drink and get high in your car. You know what can happen. If the cops stop you, you're going to jail along with them!" Following his advice caused some of my so-called guy friends to stop coming around, inviting me to their parties, or speaking to me. At the time, their actions bothered me a little but not enough to allow them to go against my uncle's warning. Just because I didn't partake in drinking or drugging, some people thought I was working for the police. They called me a "narc", which is someone who turns people into the police for doing illegal activities.

As a young person, this situation should have been disturbing to me, but I really didn't let it bother me. In fact, a good result came out of my stance on drinking. Even though some of my guy friends didn't want to hang around me, the girls all liked me! Most of my friends were girls. Eventually, the guys came around and realized I was not a "narc". I think this was because all the girls liked me, and they followed me.

In hindsight, I always say THANKS Uncle Pete for providing such great advice. His counsel sunk into my soul and strengthened my resolve. He provided me with strong threads which followed me throughout my life.

Chapter 16 - Churches

As a young boy, I had attended church most Sundays with my mother. The church was close to where we lived, so it was convenient to get to. This Pentecostal church was an all-black, small church in the neighborhood we lived in. They believed in the gifts of the Holy Spirit, meaning they spoke in tongues and performed supernatural healing through prayer. All the women wore dresses, and the men wore suits, so the environment was formal. Baptism consisted of total immersion in water. I experienced baptism when I was fairly young. Even though I attended that church until I was old enough to choose on my own, I never could speak in tongues. I guess that is a gift that I just couldn't open!

After I grew up, I attended church sporadically. My mother eventually moved from the old neighborhood and attended a Baptist church close to her new house. So I did go to that church, which was similar to the Pentecostal church. On my own, I also went to a non-denominational church, which was a multi-racial Bible-teaching church. The reason I mention this religious background is to lead you into my church experience when I visited Beth's hometown.

Beth's father, Howard, was a head usher in a very large Catholic church. So, on the Sunday we were there, the family was going to mass. They included me in that visit.

I had never visited a Catholic church, so I was not really prepared for that experience. As we pulled up to the huge, ornate historical building, I was overwhelmed by the size of the structure. Most of the churches I had attended were small, house-like buildings. This church looked like a castle!

Walking in, Howard was waiting to seat us. He proudly smiled at us and began to lead us down the long aisle. I gawked at all the people and realized I was the only black person in this congregation! Nervously, I followed Beth, her mother, and her father step-by-step down the longest aisle. It felt like miles. Finally, we got to almost the first pews, and Beth's sisters were there. Sliding into the pew, Beth whispered to me, "Just follow what we do." I thought, *What the heck does that mean?*

It wasn't long after we were seated the solemn music started and the priest came down the aisle. He wore long, ornate robes, and two young boys walked behind him. He carried an incense burner and swung it back and forth as he came down the main aisle. After he got to the altar, the mass began. During the service, the people stood up, sat down, and kneeled. Just like Beth told me to, I followed suit. I found this strange, regimented service very different from my prior church experiences.

As an adult, Beth had not been attending the Catholic Church. But she had been raised in this church, so she still remembered all the "moves". When it came time for communion, she whispered to me, "Just follow us up to the front, hold out your hand, and accept the host. But don't drink out of the cup!" I did what she said, as I was completely out of my element.

Afterward, she said, "You just had your first communion! Drinking from that cup after all those people is gross!" I guess she thought I had enough prior religious experience, so I didn't have to follow the Catholic rules of first communion. Maybe this was a violation of this church's beliefs, but that is the way she thought. And I just followed her suggestions!

After the service, her father came to us and wanted to show me the rest of the church. *What more can be in here?* I thought. He led me down a long flight of stairs into the dark basement of this huge building. It reminded me of a shadowy cave built all out of bricks and rock. Wow, there was another small chapel down in the basement. Entering the chamber, I saw plaques and candles along the walls. Howard pointed to the walls and said, "These are bishops buried here. You can light a candle and offer prayers for anything you would want."

"Really, I have never seen anything like this in a church!" I said in an awed whisper. Looking around, I counted about four people buried right in this church! What an amazing experience.

Following our departure, we returned to the house, where Howard had prepared a delicious breakfast. He was not only an usher but he loved to cook. Howard's breakfast and the warm reception by Beth's family made me feel like a special guest, further dispelling my nervousness. That was not what I had expected. After we left to return to Ohio, I was looking forward to telling my mother about this experience.

The next day dawned, and the sun was shining, creating a warm and beautiful summer day. After creeping downstairs (I was still a bit nervous), Beth informed me we were all going to the beach. Her enthusiasm for the beach immediately infused me with the spirit to get up and go. The beach was not far from the house. Climbing out of the car, I was amazed by the blueness of the lake. It was beautiful. I could feel the heat of the sand through my sandals. We laid down blankets and towels and sat down to enjoy the warmth, visit, and admire the lake. I didn't last long in the sun, as I really didn't need a tan!

Standing up, I wandered down the beach toward the water. The sand was so hot I couldn't wait to cool my feet. Squishing my toes into the wet sand offered some relief. Walking into the water made me gasp. *This water feels like ice!* I thought. I looked around and couldn't believe all the people wading and frolicking in the water. It was freezing! There were large rocks, probably 200 feet from the shore, and many people had walked or swam out to them. Some were laying on the rocks, some were jumping into the water, and some were swimming beyond the rocks. *These people have got to be crazy to go into this freezing water.*

Growing up in this neck of the woods obviously made for a very resilient person! How else could they withstand that cold water? Beth ran up to me and said, "Chester, come on in—you get used to the cold."

"I'll just watch. This water is too cold for my blood." I said as I shivered.

She laughed and proceeded to wade out to the long rocks. I watched as she climbed onto the rocks and waved at me. Before I could look away, she jumped into the deeper water and swam around like the water was a normal temperature, eventually climbing back on the rocks.

Running onto the sand from the water, we all gathered on the blankets. "That was really refreshing," Beth exclaimed.

"Ohio people just can't hang when it comes to this lake," her sister added, smiling at me. "Dad, let's make a fire."

The sun was a fiery ball sinking into the lake, causing the temperature to drop. Gathering up driftwood, Howard expertly made a fire. We all gathered around to soak up the warmth. Flo had brought sandwiches, and we all hungrily took one. Those were some of the best tasting sandwiches, sand and all! That was a good day, for sure.

Chapter 17 – The Sauna

After my first trip to Beth's hometown of Marquette, we made it back to Ohio, and I shared my experience with my mother. "Mom, there were no black people there, but everyone was pretty nice. On Sunday, we all went to a huge Catholic church. It was crazy how many people were there, and there were bodies buried in the basement!"

"Knowing Beth, I thought her family would welcome you." Mom smiled as she gently hugged me.

Laughing I replied "Yeah, I was hoping they would, but I was still nervous as heck."

"You going back ever?"

"Sure would. It was interesting and fun," I added.

As Beth and I continued building our relationship, little did I know that our initial journey up North marked the commencement of a series of such adventures. At the time, Beth worked as a waitress, and I held my laborer position at GM. After dating for a year or two, we decided to take a significant step in our relationship and move in together. While Beth had shared a place with three other girls, I resided with my Uncle Ned. However, most of our time was spent together, prompting us to merge our incomes.

I vividly recall the evenings when Beth would return home with the change and dollars she earned in tips. Together, we'd meticulously count and roll the coins. In those days, tipping was predominantly in cash, often in the form of coins. This was a far cry from the prevalent use of credit cards today. With no credit cards at our disposal, we adopted a disciplined approach to saving. Every hard-earned dollar and jingling coin brought us closer to realizing our dreams, whether they be acquiring significant possessions or traveling to new and exciting places.

My Uncle Pete and Aunt Abbie had a small house that was empty. It actually belonged to my aunt's son, but he had been sent to prison, so it was vacant. I talked to them about renting the house. My Aunt agreed but warned me once he was released, we would have to move. That was okay with me and Beth. The reason we moved in together was both an economical decision and a lifestyle decision. I was still living with my uncle, and Beth was tired of trying to live with a variety of young women. We figured if we combined our incomes, we could have a more comfortable living arrangement. And we wanted a pet. The first thing we got was an American Eskimo puppy. His name was Alaska, and he was a cute, white, fluffy dog.

In the fall, we drove up to Marquette for Thanksgiving. Beth's family had a tradition of celebrating that holiday at their camp. The camp belonged to Beth's brother-in-law, John, and her sister, Barb. This camp was in the middle of the woods, about 30 minutes outside of Marquette. The three-room camp had a freshwater stream, a Tarzan swing, and a wood-fired sauna—not to mention the acres of woods to explore and hike. Most of the guys in Beth's family used the camp as a base during deer hunting season. And deer hunting season was right before Thanksgiving, so many of the guys were already there.

The holiday was a great kick-off season for using the camp. We had the usual Thanksgiving meal and then, afterwards, some of Barb's friends came to visit—Tara, Glen, and their kids. I had never met these folks. Barb knew them from the local theater and ballet school. We were chatting and playing some card games when John said, "The sauna is ready. It's good and hot for anyone who wants to sauna." I perked up, as I had never taken a real sauna.

I went outside. The sauna was a small wooden building adjacent to the main camp. I walked in, and there was a changing room. I took my clothes off, hung them on the wall pegs, and wrapped a towel around my waist. Stepping gingerly into the steam room, I sat on one of the upper benches. Whew, it was hot. But it felt very good. As I enjoyed the warmth, I closed my eyes.

All of a sudden someone else came into the outer area of the sauna. I made sure my towel was fastened around my waist. Opening my eyes, I saw Barb's friend, Tara, and her son. I averted my eyes as they walked in because they were buck naked! I was shocked! Tara was bent over, washing her son like I wasn't even sitting five feet in front of her. In walked her husband, Glen. Glen looked at me with a wicked grin and loudly said, "Chester, why do you have a towel on? We are all family."

I stuttered and said, "Oh, that's all right. I was just leaving." I got out of there as fast as I could move. I am sure my face was red even though my skin color hid it.

I quickly got dressed and scurried back into the camp. I was laughing so hard I fell on the floor. Barb took one look at me and said, "Tara must be at it again." Everyone else was wondering what the heck was wrong with me. Barb explained about Tara. She was a theater person and considered walking around naked as sophisticated behavior. I could not believe what I had just experienced. It was not exactly what I had expected from a northern Michigan camping experience!

Chapter 18 – Upper Peninsula Travels

I found myself traveling to Marquette with Beth on a variety of occasions. Most of the trips happened during the summer. It can be treacherous driving there in the winter months—I found that out the hard way. We decided to drive up for the Christmas holidays. At the time, I had a sports car, which is not the best vehicle for snow-covered roads. We made it up, and the weather was cooperative, so we had no problems arriving for the holiday festivities.

We stayed at her parents' house until after the New Year. Her oldest sister and her husband had a New Year's Eve house party. It was great seeing all Beth's family. There was a ton of good food and many laughs. At the break of the New Year, we all danced around the house, singing and clapping along with the loud music on the stereo. We said our goodbyes later that night, as we planned on leaving early the next morning.

You have to remember this was before GPS and cell phones. We had no easy way to check the weather along our route. Heading out early that morning, the first hour wasn't bad. As we got closer to the Mackinac Bridge and Lake Michigan, snow began to fall. It wasn't long before there was no road to follow, and visibility was nil! Creeping slowly along in my little white sports car, we stopped along the road to wait. It wasn't too long before a large truck came barreling through the snow. Excitedly, Beth said, "Follow that truck!"

We crept behind the truck, letting the car tires slide through the truck tracks, and managed to get to the bridge. As we approached the bridge, you could see the storm was only on this side of it. I swear you could feel it move as we crossed it. I was pretty scared, and when we made it across the five-mile suspension bridge, I looked at Beth and said, "I will NEVER drive here again in the winter!"

That being said, I did drive up numerous times in the summer. This continued for many years, even after we got married and had kids. Most of the time, we would drive up for the 4th of July holiday. For a small town, Marquette had one of the longest parades I have ever seen. Beth's brother-in-law had purchased a 1947 Model T Ford truck. With loving care, he had restored it to look like new—bright red with a wooden truck bed. I was thrilled when he let me drive it in the parade. Many of Beth's nieces and nephews rode on the back and threw out candy. It was a very fun ride for the kids—and a memorable drive for me!

As I mentioned earlier, the town had no black residents. The nearest major city, Green Bay, Wisconsin, was known for its passionate Packers fans. In the same vein, many Marquette residents fervently supported the

Packers. At the conclusion of the parade, Beth's brother-in-law remarked, "Chet, everyone along the parade route thinks you are a Green Bay Packer!"

I chuckled in response, "Sure, I am!" It truly amused me how my stature as a big black guy made people automatically think I was a football player from Green Bay! It remains a lighthearted and amusing memory for me.

Over the years, I always looked forward to driving in the parade. Beth's brother-in-law and sister treated me like their own blood. They never hesitated to allow me to drive that wonderful old truck. That's just the way they were. We often spent time at their house, and it always amazed me how welcome they made me feel. Beth's sister used to have wild deer come to their back yard, and she would feed them. The deer loved her as much as we did. Beth's sister and husband are gone now, but the memories we created with them still live on in my heart.

Chapter 19 – The Bahamas

After moving in together, we stayed in my uncle's house for about three years. We had a dog and were starting to build a life together. We didn't always get along perfectly, but we did work together to achieve and get the things we wanted. When my uncle's stepson got out of prison, he took over the renting of the house. He wanted to increase the rent, and the place was not all that great. We had problems with the pipes freezing in the winter and water bugs in the drains. So, we started the process of finding somewhere to move.

Having a dog made it hard to find a place to rent. We talked and decided to buy a house. Now, I had a good job and Beth was a waitress. We didn't have the necessary 20% down payment on a house, so no bank would even consider giving us a mortgage loan. Plus, the interest rates were so high they limited what we could afford. After searching and looking at houses for a couple of months, we finally found a small two-bedroom house that was in our price range. It was not perfect, but it was acceptable, and we figured it was better than renting. We weren't married yet, but we made an economic decision to buy a house together. A local savings and loan bank agreed to loan us the money. We became happy homeowners!

Ever since we lived together, we always put our money together and saved it so we could work toward our goals.

My mother once called and asked, "Chester, do you and Beth want to go to the Bahamas? We have a group organizing a charter plane in April."

"Let me ask Beth. That would be fun. I have never been anywhere like that."

After I talked to Beth, we decided to go. We had been saving money for a while now, and the trip was something we could afford.

When it was time to go, we boarded our dog, packed our bags, and went to the airport with Mother. This was a charter plane, so everyone on board was in our group. The majority of the people were ladies. Now, this was the era of airplane flights where you always got meals. So, as we got on the plane, the pilot made an announcement: "Ladies and Gentlemen, we are having a delay as the meals have not yet been loaded. We have an option for you all to make a decision on. Would you forgo meals for free drinks all the way to Nassau?"

A cheer arose from the entire plane. Except there was my cry, "Nooo, I want some food!" They heard me. Someone from the airline got a sandwich on the plane to appease me! Everyone else was quite happy with the drinks!

As we were coming into Nassau, the pilot opened his door and invited anyone to come up front and view the island from the front windshield. Now, this would never be allowed in this day and age. Many of the ladies, feeling a bit tipsy, carefully walked to the cockpit. Some ladies even sat on the pilot's lap. Everyone took pictures. I was a little worried, as this was my first time flying. Most of the ladies were pretty heavy, and with all that weight up front, I couldn't wait until they sat down! The pilot was turning the plane and tilting it so the women could get pictures. In my mind's eye, I imagined the plane doing a nosedive because of all the weight in the front! Pleadingly, I thought, *Please sit down so we don't crash!*

We landed just fine, despite my misgivings, and checked into the hotel. My mother was rooming with her girlfriend. After getting something to eat, Mother said, "We're going to the casino. See you a bit later." Well, the whole week we were there, we only saw Mother a couple of times. She and her friend pretty much lived at the casinos.

Beth and I did the normal tourist stuff—sunbathing, swimming, shopping, and just taking in the sights. On one of our excursions to the straw market, we walked by some natives squatting by some dirty looking water. They had a couple of pots and were using the dirty water to make some sort of food. It all looked very disgusting.

"Hey what's that you got?" I asked.

"We cookin', man," they answered.

"No, you're not. Come over here with us," I said. They cautiously got up and walked with us. I took them into the local market and got them some meat and cheese and water.

"Thanks, man," they all said in unison. We felt a bit sick thinking about what they were going to eat before we came along. In our country, dogs eat better food than what those Bahamians were going to eat.

On the final day of our trip, we noticed Mother and her friend seated by the pool. This was a duo we had scarcely encountered throughout the entire week. Smiling at them, I asked, "Hey, what's up with you two? Did you get breakfast yet?"

To my surprise, Mother quietly confessed, "We lost all our money in the casino."

Grateful for the fortunate timing of our presence, I couldn't help but reflect on what might have happened had we not accompanied them on this journey. We immediately took them both out for a meal and provided some spending money to tide them over until we returned home. If I remember correctly, they chose to revisit the casino with the funds we provided. Fortunately, luck was on their side this time, and they returned home with a modest amount of money.

Chapter 20 – Bahamas Again

A few years later, we again decided to visit the Bahamas. This trip was planned with my good friend, Mike, and his wife, Sharon. This was our first trip with another couple. We planned and organized our stay together at an all-inclusive resort. Leaving from Cleveland airport, our anticipation for a relaxing and entertaining week ahead was palpable.

Landing in Nassau, with the sun glinting off the crystal blue water, we hustled through the airport to find a bus from the hotel awaiting us. Breathlessly, we arrived at the hotel, checked in, and immediately headed out to the Nassau straw markets. Now, the straw markets are a popular attraction in the Bahamas where you have to barter for your wares. Beth outdid herself in the bartering arena. I felt like I had to tear her away from that place or we would not have any room for our clothes on the return trip home.

Back at the resort, we examined the itinerary for the day and discovered it was time for happy hour at the resort. We met and mingled with many other young couples from all over the world. After a few drinks and conch fritters (a staple of the island), Mike asked, "Who's up for dinner?"

Three other couples said, in unison, "We are starving. Let's go!"

Strolling down the street, we decided on a local restaurant that looked quaint. We all were seated, and some of us were brave enough to try some local dishes. One guy ordered turtle soup. I decided to play it safe and order a hamburger. When our meals were delivered, the smell that emanated from the turtle soup was so strong and fishy it made us all gag. Despite the stench, all of our food was devoured in record time.

The next day dawned, and after a hearty breakfast, we headed out to the casino. Beth and I are not gamblers, but that day we decided to give the slots a try. Our money seemed to last for hours. Of course, the free drinks were welcomed by all except me. I was always the designated driver as I did not consume alcohol. Even though I prefer Beth not to drink, I could not impose my beliefs on her—she is her own person.

After a few hours, Mike and Sharon, slurring their words, said "We are busted. Let's go." Beth, a bit tipsy, agreed with them.

Smiling at the three of them, I laughingly announced, "Okay, but I made up for all of your losses. I won! You have to know when to hold them, know when to fold them, just like the Kenny Rogers song!"

All three of them looked at me and shouted, "You don't have to rub it in!"

Arriving back at the hotel, we all went to our rooms, as it was late. We had been in our room for about ten minutes when we started hearing some strange sounds and words coming through the wall. A female voice said, "Come on, bring it down, come on, come on, bring the hanger down." What the heck were we hearing? Then we heard a male voice responding, "Here it comes, here it comes—you're going to reach the sky."

I looked at Beth, she looked at me, and we both burst out laughing as we realized we were hearing some type of copulation. Sure enough, it wasn't long after that we heard a bump-bump-bump sound of a bed hitting against the hotel wall. Luckily, we were so tired the sound didn't keep us awake.

The next day brought another round of partying at the hotel. At happy hour, many young couples mingled, enjoying the drinks and merriment. Of course, because of what we had heard the previous night, I was curious who was staying in the room next to ours. Walking around the room, I asked everyone I met if they were in that room next to us. It wasn't until I came upon a newlywed couple that I found my answer. They said, "Yes, that's our room. Why do you ask?"

Looking serious as I could, I responded, "Well, we are adults, so I'm just going to tell you what we heard last night. The walls were coming down in our room with the banging from your room, and someone sounded like they were crying a tear! I really would like to know what kind of recipe you were using in there!" As soon as I said this, the newlyweds both turned as red as a ripe apple. Everyone burst out laughing, including the newlyweds.

Later on, we went to the pool and just hung out and relaxed. The next morning, we had an excursion planned on the Yellow Bird boat. After boarding the boat, we all settled in for the short day trip to a small island. We were greeted upon arrival by many servers who offered us drinks and showed us the amenities offered during our stay. There were lovely hammocks strung between the banana trees, snorkeling was offered in the bay, and food was being prepared in a way we had never witnessed—cooked underground with hot coals.

I tried snorkeling for the first time, and it was a beautiful experience until I saw a large fish. "What kind of fish is that?" I asked the guide.

"Oh, that's a baby shark," he replied.

"What? I thought the reef was supposed to keep out sharks!" I shouted.

The guide replied, "It's just a baby, and sometimes they get through."

I immediately jumped out of the water and was done with my snorkeling experience.

Sharon and Mike were snorkeling together around the base of the boat. "Hey, there's a baby shark out there," I shouted to them. They just looked up and ignored my warning. No one else seemed to care about the baby shark. *Oh well*, I thought, *I tried to warn them*. It wasn't too long after that Sharon popped up and yelled, "Forget the shark. I just found a diamond ring!"

Everyone came around as she showed us the large, sparkling diamond ring in her hand. What a treasure to find! The guide said, "It's yours. You find, you keep."

Sharon was ecstatic and said, "I know just what to do with this, too. My sister wants a diamond ring, and she will buy it!" How many people get a souvenir on their vacation that way?

The servers started hollering the food was ready, so come and get it. Hot packets of foil were dug up from the ground, and the steaming fresh grouper and vegetables were so delicious. We all ate until our bellies could hold no more. Moving away from the food, we lay in the hammocks to soak up the late afternoon sun and relax. Lying in the hammock, gazing at the clear blue sky, I thought, *This is the life, for sure.*

Chapter 21 - Sports

One of other attractions that Beth and I enjoyed besides traveling and music was sports. I know that many women are not that fond of sporting events, so I truly appreciated this mutual enjoyment we shared. Our relationship has managed to survive, despite many challenges caused by our own doings, because we value and enjoy these shared experiences.

Early on when we began dating, I played softball on a men's team. Besides playing ball, I eventually became president of the women's softball league in our area. Back then, we had a large league consisting of twenty women's teams. I also coached one of the teams first sponsored by a local restaurant, Red Barn, and later sponsored by the Shrine Club. This team had a variety of ladies ranging in age from 17 to 40. Competing all over Ohio, the ladies even won the very first Stroh's Beer softball tournament in Greenwich, Ohio. We also won the local league for two years in a row.

Over the course of six years, it was not always easy to coach the wide range of personalities on the team, but I really loved the challenge. To this day, I love softball and find great enjoyment in following the adventures of our great nieces and nephews who play the sport.

While I was busy with coaching, playing, and administering the league, Beth was one of the scorekeepers. She had never done this before but quickly learned the ins and outs of the necessary skills for tracking strikes, balls, hits, and errors. One season, during our team practice, I asked, "Beth, do you want to try out for the team?"

Looking up from her perch on the bleachers, Beth answered, "Well, I can try. Never played before, but maybe I can do it." She went into the locker room and changed into one of our stylish uniforms—shorts, shirt, and a baseball hat.

Looking cute, she walked to the outfield and put on a glove to prepare for catching. Now, I hit the ladies pop ups and grounders all the time so they could practice for perfection. I called to Beth, "Sweetheart, I'm going to hit a couple of pop ups so you can try to catch them." Of course, I only hit an easy pop up, not too high, for her to catch. Beth gazed up in the sky and raised her glove to catch the pop up. Plop went the softball as it hit her directly on the head!

"Are you okay?" I shouted.

More embarrassed than hurt, Beth shook her head. Walking off the field, she said, "I'm sticking to keeping score. Softball is not for me!" In my head, I was silently laughing, even though I was really glad she did not get hurt. But that was the end of Beth's softball career!

High school sports were another area Beth and I enjoyed following. We would attend football and basketball games, hoping all the time our local teams would be talented enough to make the state playoffs. In 1980, a local Catholic high school made it to the state basketball championships. We followed the team to Columbus, enjoying the frenzied fans and the talented, competitive play of each game. As an added bonus, our local team won the championship, and we thoroughly enjoyed the celebration. It's always fun to win!

Over the next few years, after that first experience, we were hooked on the excitement and attended many state tournaments. During the first tournament, Beth was enamored by the scalping of tickets. The smaller size of St. John's arena made for a perfect venue for the resale of game tickets.

Throughout basketball season, we vigilantly monitored teams that showed promise of making it to the tournaments. If the location wasn't too far away, we would embark on drives to buy tickets directly available from the schools competing in the games in Columbus. This strategic approach not only ensured access to game tickets if the chosen team advanced but also presented opportunities for us to enhance our seating arrangements. Additionally, by engaging in scalping and ticket trading, we managed not only to secure better seating but also generate some extra income, effectively offsetting the costs of our four-day stay in Columbus. I still vividly remember the time Beth managed to sell a five dollar floor ticket for $50!

For an extended period, we reveled in the excitement of the basketball competitions, actively participating in the thrill of the tournaments. Columbus, with its plethora of eateries lining High Street in the heart of the Ohio State campus, became an integral part of our experience. Having restaurant options close by added to the fun and gave us time to relax away from the hectic ticket scalping during the games.

However, the landscape underwent a significant transformation when the university built a new, larger basketball facility. While the increased capacity allowed more spectators to attend, it also signaled a shift in the dynamics of ticket scalping. The once lucrative venture lost much of its allure in the face of the expansive new venue, and I couldn't help but think, *So much for progress!*

Chapter 22 – Meeting my Father

Having spent my entire adult life in Ohio, I had never had the chance to meet my birth father. We had left Mississippi when I was just a toddler, and I had no recollection of him whatsoever. The revelation came when I was 27 years old; my mother sat me down and posed a question that caught me off guard, "Chester, would you like to meet your father?"

Immediately, I replied, "Of course, I would. I never thought there would be a chance to find him."

With a warm smile, she added, "I have his phone number. If you're interested, I could set up a visit. You can take the train, and I'll even purchase the ticket for you!"

It was obvious she knew how I felt about finding my father. This was her way of helping me know the other side of my family. My younger brother was also his son, but there was no way he could go as he was in college. It was decided I would travel by train to Meridian, Mississippi, and my father would pick me up.

A few days later, I excitedly boarded the train. Settling into my seat, I made myself comfortable for the long couple of days rumbling toward the south. After two long days of travel, we arrived at the train station. I quickly climbed out onto the platform and scanned the area. My father was supposed to pick me up, but I did not know what he looked like. I walked around the area, checking out all the black men who were at the station. After what seemed like an eternity, a tall black man approached me and inquired, "Are you Chester?"

"Yes."

"Follow me," he said as he took my suitcase and ambled toward the parking lot.

As I settled into the car, he introduced himself, "My name is June. I'm your father. How was the trip from Ohio?"

Without hesitation, I replied, "It was long, but I enjoyed the scenery. Plus, I had a sleeper, so it was comfortable. Thanks for picking me up. It's great to finally meet you."

He started the car and drove toward his home. From that point on, he highlighted various points of interest along the route. Other than that, he didn't say much until we reached the house.

After walking into his home, he introduced me to his wife. She welcomed me and gave me a hug. My father looked me in the eyes and said, "Sorry, I gotta go back to work, but you can stay here and meet the rest of my family. I'll be back in a day or two." With some dismay,

I discovered he drove semi trucks and was often on the road for many days at a time.

His wife and I chatted easily, filling each other in on the details of our lives. I found out I had two sisters and three brothers. It was almost dinner time, and to my delight, in walked all my siblings except one sister who was working. There was a knock on the door, and more relatives came walking in. I met more uncles, aunts, and cousins then I ever thought I had! My grandfather told me how he used to carry me on his back when he was plowing the field. Now, how could I not remember that? Soon, dinner was ready, and while we ate, stories flowed. Before I knew it, my brothers wanted to take me out to a local pub.

Immediately upon arriving at the club, my brothers wanted me to buy a round of drinks. "I'll buy you all drinks, but I don't drink. I'll have my usual cranberry juice!"

"You're kidding," they said in unison.

"No, I'm not," I replied as I ordered a round. "Let's toast!"

Sitting down and observing my brothers, I realized they were already a bit drunk. They began fraternizing with many of the people in the bar who seemed to be from the local neighborhood. In walked a beautiful young lady, who sat down close to me. She smiled at me and said, "Hi, my name is Amy. Do you mind if I sit here?"

"No problem. I'm Chester. I just got here, and I'm visiting my family for the first time. This is my first time in this area, and I'll be here for a few days."

She was surprised by that, and we started talking about this and that. She was mesmerizing and very interesting to talk to. I was very much attracted to her—she was smart and beautiful. Suddenly, she asked, "Hey, do you want me to show you some of the sights around town?" I quickly said, "Yeah, let's go."

My brothers were preoccupied with all their friends and hadn't paid me much attention since we arrived. The bar was near my father's house, so I didn't tell them I was leaving.

We drove around and talked for a bit. Amy told me she was a nurse and loved her job. In turn, I told her what I did. We grabbed some fast food and talked some more. After a bit, she said, "This has been fun Chester. Let's do this again, okay?" I agreed. She dropped me off back at the bar, and I found my brothers there, still partying with the locals.

We all returned back to the house, and I went immediately to bed. It had been a long, adventurous day meeting so many new relatives and friends.

When I woke up that morning, I looked forward to another day with my father's family. My father was supposed to arrive later, so I got up and quietly went into the living room. There was no one else there, so I turned on the TV. I heard my father's wife in the kitchen. She was talking to someone. As I was sitting there wondering who was out there, Amy walked into the room and looked at me. Shocked, she exclaimed, "What are you doing here?"

Just as shocked, I repeated, "What are you doing here?"

She immediately said, "This is my family. Are you my brother visiting from Sandusky?"

With a sinking heart, I realized the truth. Amy was my sister. This truth definitely changed my feelings toward her. I got up and hugged her and laughingly said, "I sure am glad you found me here today instead of what we had planned for tonight!"

She looked me in the eye and said, "Welcome home, brother!"

The remainder of my visit was very pleasant with no more surprises. I enjoyed sitting with my father and getting to know him. He seemed to be a hard-working, family-oriented man. After I returned to Ohio, I tried to stay in touch with him. Three years after I met him, he was killed while he was driving a semi in a tornado. To this day, I am so very thankful I connected with him when I did. With my birth father getting killed so young, I think God gave me the grace to know him before he was called home.

Chapter 23 – Family Reunions

After meeting my father and his family, I stayed in touch with various siblings, aunts, uncles, and cousins. Most of them welcomed me into the family with open arms. Happily, I truly enjoyed the interactions and found myself looking forward to getting to know my father's people. Theirs was a large extended family, and they had big family reunions I looked forward to attending.

I journeyed to the first reunion on my own in Meridian, Mississippi. There, I again socialized with my brothers and sisters. I met many cousins, but the one I really connected with was a schoolteacher who had one daughter. Her name was Dorie, and she even came to visit me in Sandusky after the initial reunion. Beth and I welcomed Dorie and her daughter, Alice, into our house. I even found out I had an aunt close by in Detroit.

Over the years, I've attended a handful of reunions in various cities, including Chicago, Detroit, and Baltimore. Each gathering was a tapestry of relatives, with so many faces and stories it was a challenge to keep them all straight in my head. At one of the reunions, one of the aunts who lived in California unveiled a fascinating piece of our family history—a genealogy scroll that extended an impressive 25 feet. This detailed and intricate record traced the descendants of our patriarch, George, who had been born a slave. George, my great-

great-grandfather, was born on a plantation and named after the owner.

According to my grandfather, George was a very common name, so much so that the debts of individuals with the same name became entangled. In an effort to correct this misappropriation and to distinguish himself from the other Georges, George's owner adopted the surname of Granger. This decision not only set our family on a unique trajectory but also bestowed upon my great-great-grandfather the surname of Granger.

The son of George, Judge George Granger, was born in Panola, Alabama. Judge, my great-grandfather, was an extremely valuable slave. He was valued at $1,500 and was kept out of the civil war because of his ability as a timber man. As told by my grandfather, Judge was capable of cutting 20,000 feet of pine and 8,000 feet of oak per day. Despite the extreme amount of work imposed upon Judge, he managed to establish a family, which is a testament to his spirit.

Judge married a 15-year old slave girl, Mariah, who was said to be the daughter of a mixed race mother and Geronimo, a Native American. My great-grandfather's wife was the product of rape. Her mother was washing clothes by the river in Panalo, Alabama, and Geronimo came upon her when he had been imprisoned and violated her. The baby, Mariah, had long, flowing hair and was sold into slavery at the age of five.

Following her marriage to Judge, Mariah's journey took on new dimensions. She embraced not only being a wife but also became a midwife. Together, Mariah and Judge produced and raised fifteen children, providing a living testament to their resilience and love. Among their offspring was my grandfather, Hervie, a remarkable soul who embodied the strength and fortitude of his parents' marriage. It was through Hervie that I glimpsed a piece of my family's history, meeting him for the first time when I met my father. Hervie was an example of strength in the face of adversity, living for an impressive 103 years.

These reunions were not just gatherings for socialization; they provided portals into a rich tapestry of our shared history. The genealogy scroll, the shared stories, and the meeting of family members added layers of significance to our family name. Even though I did not share the same surname as my father's family, we had the same roots, and the reunions allowed for exploration and celebration of the remarkable journey that brought us together.

Chapter 24 – My First Son

I always had a true passion for roller skating. Sandusky had a popular rink where all the young guys went to not only skate but to meet and socialize with girls. Skating to the rhythmic beats of the popular music of the day, I honed my skills and became adept at dancing on skates. Of course, this helped greatly to attract the attention of several young ladies. I even obtained a side job helping at the rink. This gave me free access to skating plus provided extra money for my pocket.

During a visit to an out-of-town skating rink, I crossed paths with a young lady, leading to a brief yet intense relationship. This connection resulted in the birth of my baby son, Link. We did not get married, but I remained committed to supporting my son financially. Despite the distance of about 45 minutes between us, I made an effort to see him and spend time with him as much as I could.

As the years passed, Link's mother lost custody, and he became a ward of the court. This was an undoubtedly distressing and precarious situation for any child. Despite the challenging circumstances, I continued to provide support. In retrospect, I realize I should have pursued custody, but at the time, my living conditions were not stable enough to offer him a suitable home.

Years later, when I first met Beth, long after the birth of my son, I immediately told her about my parental responsibilities. Beth embraced the situation, wholeheartedly, meeting Link whenever he came to visit. Her understanding and acceptance alleviated my concerns about having a son from a previous relationship. I found her support incredibly valuable, considering that not all women would be as accepting of a child from an earlier liaison. Beth's understanding and openness made a significant difference, reinforcing the strength of our connection and creating a positive environment for both my son and me. Little did I realize how important her acceptance would be to our continued relationship in the coming years.

A few years after we bought the house together, the court approached me to see if I was interested in taking my son full-time. I was immediately open to this idea, but I told the woman I had to ask my girlfriend. After discussing this with Beth, we decided to give it a try. After all, he was living with his 80-year-old grandmother, and she was not capable of keeping up with an 11-year-old boy. Every time he came to visit me, there was an evident lack of care in both his body and his clothing. I understood not having the stability of family. Even though I had my mother, not having a father made me realize how important that role is to a young boy.

I called the social worker. "Hi, we are willing to give it a try. What do we have to do next?"

"We have to come and discuss this with both of you. Also, we want to make sure your home is adequate," she replied.

"Okay, when can you come?" We scheduled a visit. Beth and I were both pretty excited about this new experience. As much as I can remember, the social worker explained how the move would happen. She did not seem to be bothered by the fact we were not married. The court's attitude showed us how precarious and unstable Link's living situation was.

A few years before Link moved in with us, I found out I had another son, Joe. Joe was the same age as Link! I didn't know for sure if Joe was my son, but my mother told me, "He's yours, Chester." So, I took her word as truth. Joe had been raised by his mother and her husband, so I was not really in his life when he was a baby. At the time, he was not really doing well with his mother, who was divorced. I asked Beth if we should try to get him and raise the two boys together. Well, that did not go over well with his mother. She resented me trying to get him, and she also did not like the idea of Beth getting involved with her son. It was too bad because maybe Joe could have benefited from living with us.

When Link moved in with us, there was some trepidation on his part. This was to be expected because he was moving to a new town and a new home. There were a few nights where he ended up crying himself to sleep. In hindsight, we should have got him some counseling. But you know, back then mental health was not discussed or recognized as a need. We did the best we could by ourselves to help him adjust. Years later, Link told me he initially thought he was coming to visit for the weekend when he moved into our house. No wonder he was upset. Why did the social worker not explain this to us or him?

Link was 11 years old and in the sixth grade when he came to us. Because he was moving to a brand new school and city, we had to get him tested and evaluated in order to enroll him in the proper class levels for our local school system. To our dismay, we discovered his reading level was not what it should be. A tutor was recommended to us by the school system. Luckily, the tutor was very helpful, and after a few years, Link was reading at the correct academic level.

Eventually, he adjusted to living with us. Most of the time, he did well and developed into a well-mannered young man. He took part in football and wrestling in high school.

We wanted him to go to college, but his heart led him into military service. He seemed to enjoy the discipline imposed by the armed forces. He attended two basic trainings, both the Army and the Marines, and ended up joining the toughest branch of the military—the Marines. I remember he went through hell during basic training. Some of the letters he wrote showed us how tough they were on him, both mentally and physically. Despite the extreme challenges, Link seemed to thrive in the Marines. He made a career out of serving our country. What an accomplishment!

Chapter 25 – An Amazing Trip

Three years into my marriage with Beth, we planned an amazing month-long trip around the United States with her parents. In order to book the trip, we contacted a travel agency, and they arranged our tickets on Amtrak and reservations at hotels for our various destinations. Travel back then was more difficult to arrange because there was no internet, so we had to rely on the services of the travel agent. That being said, early one morning, we excitedly boarded the train in Sandusky, Ohio, with our tickets in hand and headed for our trip to various points out west. Our first stop was in Chicago, Illinois, at Union Station to catch the train which would transport us across the country to our first destination: Phoenix, Arizona.

It just so happened that Beth was three months pregnant with our first child during this trip. She wasn't showing yet, so no one other than us knew she was expecting. The trip to Chicago was uneventful as we chugged across Ohio into Illinois. Union Station is a huge, busy train station, so we had plenty to explore during the three-hour wait for our connection.

Boarding the train bound for the west, we found ourselves in coach seats, a decision that, in hindsight, seemed quite naïve given Beth's parents' age. Flo and Howard, both in their 70s, were remarkably healthy and active, but the prospect of a three-day journey across the country should have warranted a sleeper car. It is ironic now that I am around that age, I would never travel on a train for that distance without a sleeper!

As the train traversed through numerous states, we settled into our seats, enjoying the ever-changing scenery outside our windows. When you travel on Amtrak, there are many stops on the journey. Most of the stops are short, so you cannot depart the train. At the longer stops, we welcomed the chance to get off the train and stretch our legs. Other than those stops, we entertained ourselves by chatting with the other travelers, going to the dining car, snacking, and playing cards. Our interaction with the other passengers provided a diversity of characters, each with their own tales and experiences. After two days of the monotony of a sedentary lifestyle, I found myself performing impromptu sit-ups in the middle of the aisle! Not only did this provide me some relief from inaction, but it provided unexpected amusement for our fellow passengers.

On the third day of travel, with much anticipation, we reached our first destination of Phoenix. Beth's brother, who lived in Phoenix with his wife and three children, picked us up at the train station. This was my first time in the southwest, so as we traveled through the city, I was amazed by the massive mountains and lush foliage. After we arrived at his home, we had a great time visiting with the kids and enjoying the sunny climate.

During our stay, we toured the city and traveled to Apache Junction, a small retirement community close by the Superstition Mountains, to visit with an old friend of Flo and Howard.

Our last day in Phoenix dawned bright, sunny, and hot as usual, and the kids had to go to school. Considering the school was only two blocks away, Howard and I decided to walk them. Howard had been walking around the yard, shirtless, with just his pants on. Imagine an older, shirtless, white man and a young black man walking three little white kids to school. What a picture we must have been!

After our stay in Phoenix, we boarded the train for a day trip and headed for Oceanside, California. I was looking forward to this segment of our trip as my son, Link, was stationed close by in Camp Pendleton, and we would see him during our stay. We were all anticipating visiting Oceanside because it is a beautiful city along the Pacific Ocean, and from what we had heard, it was a great place to enjoy and relax.

Arriving at our hotel, we were all enthralled by the beauty of the area. During our stay, we enjoyed strolling along the quaint streets and visiting the popular Oceanside Pier. The panoramic views of the ocean took my breath away. I can still smell the salty sea breeze which invigorated my senses, and I can hear the seagulls cawing adding to a coastal ambiance.

After we spent a few days in Oceanside, Link paid us a visit at our hotel. He extended a warm invitation to explore Camp Pendleton, offering us an exclusive tour of the base. This immersive experience allowed us to explore the various facilities and view military aircraft, helicopters, tanks, and various other vehicles used by the Marines. Link guided us through the base, sharing the historical sites commemorating the Marine Corps' legacy. We had the privilege of visiting memorials, museums, and historical landmarks.

The following day, we rented a car to make the trek to Tijuana, Mexico. We all piled into the car for the short drive to the Mexican border. The drive was quick, and the border passage was easy—no need to show passports, so much different than today. The day was extremely hot, and the area heading into Tijuana resembled a third-world country. There were women and children lining the road, sitting in the hot sun, begging for money. It was extremely sad to see the children running up to people, pleading for money while the mothers seemed to be asleep or passed out in the heat.

We parked the car and began walking into the downtown area of Tijuana. The streets were crowded, and people bustled about trying to find the best bargains. Beth and

Flo ended up bartering with the various vendors to get some heavy woolen blankets. It seemed crazy to be buying such a warm blanket when the temperatures were soaring around us. As we trudged back to the car, Beth began feeling sick to her stomach—she was pregnant, and the excessive heat did not agree with her. It was near impossible to find a place to get water, but right by where we parked was a McDonald's. I have never been so happy to see those golden arches. After refreshing ourselves with water, we happily left the land of Tijuana.

We were scheduled to leave Oceanside the next evening. Link dropped us off at the train station, said his goodbyes, and wished us well on the next leg of our journey. We were all excited as we looked forward to heading up the coast of California—all the way to San Francisco. As we eagerly awaited the train, soon the time to leave passed. Confused and worried, we located a pay phone in order to call Amtrak and find out what was going on.

"We were scheduled to leave at 5:00PM today, and the train never showed up."

The Amtrak service representative checked the station and time and replied, "I'm sorry, sir, there was no train scheduled for that station. There was a bus scheduled to leave for Los Angeles."

"Oh no!" I exclaimed. "Now what should we do?"

She went on, "There is a bus that comes through early in the morning you could catch. Other than that, there is no other train or bus scheduled."

Thanking her, I hung up and went back to where Beth and her parents were waiting.

When I explained our predicament to them, horrified looks swept across on all their faces. Stranded at the train depot, we found ourselves without a means of leaving. Link was back at Camp Pendleton, which left us with no transportation. After carefully weighing our options, which were not many, the only choice we had was to wait outside at the depot.

Settling in for the night on the cold benches, we were fortunate to have our blankets we had purchased in Tijuana. As I patrolled the area, I noticed a few homeless individuals hanging around. The homeless individuals walked close by where we were sitting, gazing at our possessions. I kept a vigilant eye on them, pretending I had something under my coat, recognizing the potential threat they posed to us. Sleep eluded me that night, but with perseverance and luck, we all managed to make it through.

All during that night, I had been pretty scared, but with false bravado I stared and walked back and forth, keeping the strange homeless people away. Finally, the bus arrived early in the morning. Tired but relieved, we boarded the bus which would take us to the Los Angeles train depot. I immediately fell into a deep sleep. It seemed like a few minutes passed, then we arrived.

The LA depot loomed before us, a once-grand structure now marred by neglect. The grandeur of its architecture seemed to have surrendered to a state of disrepair, with overflowing trash, dirty floors, and restrooms in need of a deep cleaning. We eagerly left behind the disgusting facility, anticipating the upcoming journey on the train bound for San Francisco.

As we embarked on our coastal route, the scenery unfolded in a breathtaking display. The rocky coastline, covered with abundant foliage, painted a breathtaking picture of natural beauty. Experiencing the decaying train station made us appreciate the vibrant landscape even more. Arriving in San Francisco, we found our hotel and made plans for our stay in the golden city.

During our stay in San Francisco, we explored many of the typical touristy spots. We navigated the city's iconic hills to enjoy the charm of Fisherman's Wharf. Amid the many eateries, we indulged in a delightful lunch. The highlight of this segment of our trip was an expedition to the giant redwoods. By renting a car, we embarked on a scenic drive along the coastline, eventually climbing a mountain to arrive at a park which did have some medium-sized redwoods. I was eager to view the huge redwoods that you can drive your car through. After asking a park ranger where the huge redwoods were, he laughingly informed me we would have to drive another three hours to encounter those majestic trees. Realizing the considerable distance involved, we opted to appreciate the beauty of the park we were already in, relishing—with some regret—the beauty of the smaller redwoods.

The drive back down the mountain, though scenic, was a bit treacherous, and I was relieved to arrive back onto the level highway. After this excursion, our journey was nearing its completion. Our next leg was to board the train that would take us back across the country to Ohio. The following day, we left San Francisco behind and traversed through the beauty of Colorado. The narrated train ride provided us with not only terrific scenery but also the history of the region.

After returning to Ohio, we reflected on our recent adventure and concluded that, despite a few travel hiccups, it had been a truly wonderful trip. In hindsight, I am immensely grateful for the opportunity to travel with Beth's parents. Although they are no longer with us, the memories we created, the adventures we experienced, and the precious time shared were truly priceless. This journey also taught me about the strength of bonds and the resilience we find in overcoming challenges together and finding humor in every situation.

Chapter 26 – Police Brutality

Several years into our marriage, Beth worked quite a distance away from our home here in Sandusky. On a day when I was at home, recovering from a recent heart procedure, I decided to surprise her. Early in the morning, I took Beth's car to get her some coffee and fill up the tank before she hit the road.

However, my plans took an unexpected turn. On my way to the gas station, a police officer pulled me over. Stepping up to my car, he sternly instructed me to step out. Confused, I complied, meeting his gaze with uncertainty. Abruptly, he demanded my license. As I reached into my pocket, apparently not quickly enough for him, he seized my arm, barking, "Hands on top of the vehicle—now!"

In that moment, he forcefully twisted my arm behind my back. "What did I do?" I yelled. Instead of an explanation, he shoved me into the back of the police cruiser, commanding me to stay silent. Leaving me in the cruiser, he walked over to the gas station. I observed him talking to the manager and making a phone call. He must have called for a tow truck because, eventually, one arrived.

In utter horror, I watched the tow truck hauling my wife's car away. Panic surged through me as I grappled with the urgent need to let her know what was going on.

Desperation in my voice, I repeated, "Why did you stop me? I wasn't speeding." He said nothing, just pulled out and headed for the police station. Upon our arrival, he pulled me out, slapped on handcuffs, and escorted me into a cell.

Time dragged on, each moment feeling like an eternity, until he finally allowed me to call my wife. In a state of shock, my recollection of that conversation is faint. I vaguely recall urging her to go to work, promising to explain everything later. Eventually, they released me with some type of hyped-up resisting arrest charge.

Beth spent the entire day at work, oblivious to the turmoil that had transpired. She had no way of contacting me until she returned home that evening. Once we sat down, I finally unraveled the unsettling events of the morning. Hearing my disturbing tale, Beth was incredulous. We decided I would go to court and fight these trumped-up charges.

The next day, telling my son Link about my experience, he asked the police officer's name. When I told him, he started laughing and declared, "Dad, that was payback!"

Puzzled, I asked him, "What are you talking about?"

Link proceeded to tell me the police officer was the same person he had defeated multiple times in high school wrestling. He was surprised I didn't remember him. Link added, "I beat him every time we wrestled. I kept him from going to State." Now, it was my turn to be incredulous.

It was difficult to fathom that a police officer could be so petty and unprofessional. Refusing to accept the unfounded accusation against me, I decided to take a stand. Returning to the gas station where it had all happened, the manager, who had observed the whole incident, agreed to testify to what she saw. She composed a statement supporting the truth of what had transpired.

When I arrived at court, I felt confident that the charges against me would be dismissed. The police officer presented his version—filled with lies. When I was telling the judge what had happened on the day of my arrest, his eyes widened. Next, I shared the written testimony of the gas station manager. Without any hesitation, the judge immediately threw out the charges. The debacle was finally behind me.

In today's world, incidents like these often find their way onto video. It may have even gone viral. This could empower individuals to take legal action against unjust policing. In our case, we had to pay to retrieve my wife's impounded car, a cost we bore silently. At the time, we didn't even think about retaliation. We pressed down the trauma and resumed our daily lives. Several years later, I learned the same police officer was fired from our local police department for corrupt practices. It was reported he pulled people over and extorted money from them instead of ticketing them. Upon hearing this tale, my immediate thought was maybe this was karma following through on my behalf.

Chapter 27 – A Fall

The winter of 2016 ushered a wave of challenges and changes into my world. My two youngest sons, Nate and Nic, had ventured to different areas of the country—Nate was working and living in vibrant Las Vegas, and Nic was in his second year of college. Consequently, it was just Beth and me, two solitary figures living in the empty nest of our home.

Earlier that morning, Beth had left for work, leaving me alone in the embrace of a typical Ohio winter day. The air was frigid, with only a smattering of snow along the edges of the roads. Being retired, I found myself with ample time on my hands and decided to venture outside to check the mail. As I ambled down the driveway, the winter chill touched my face. Intent on reaching the mailbox, I started to cross the road. However, fate had a different plan. Before I could even take more than a couple of steps, my feet betrayed me, slipping out from under me. In an instant, my body flew up in the air, and I crash-landed on my back.

It was a moment that felt surreal, as if I were a cartoon character who had stepped on a banana skin and soared in the air! Shocked and winded, I lay there, staring up at the winter sky. Surprisingly, there was no immediate pain, but a singular thought ran through my mind: I can't get up!

After what seemed an eternity—but was more like 15 minutes—my neighbor came outside. "Chester, are you alright?" he shouted.

"I can't get up. Can you help me?" I implored. He ran over to get another neighbor to help pick me up. With much grunting and pulling, they managed to get me on my feet. They helped me into the house and lowered me into a chair.

"I can't move my hands," I shouted.

"Let me help you get your coat off," my one neighbor said.

I was trembling and scared. "What am I going to do if I can't use my hands?"

My neighbor replied, "Don't worry. I'll call Beth." Luckily, Beth answered right away and said she would be home in ten minutes.

Breathless, Beth arrived in the house, and after hearing what had happened, said, "We have to get to the ER to get you examined."

Luckily, I could walk, and Beth helped me get into the car. Arriving at the hospital, I was immediately taken in for x-rays. At this point, my neck was quite sore, but I was able to move my hands again. After a battery of tests, a doctor arrived and looked at me. Without much preamble, he announced I need surgery immediately or I would end up like the man who played Superman. Beth's eyes widened when he said this. I was shocked.

"Wait a minute," said Beth, "we are not doing any surgery today."

I agreed with her and said, "Yes, we want to get a second opinion. Maybe therapy can help."

The doctor could only agree with us and said he would get the release papers prepared. Leaving there, we contacted a doctor who could refer me for therapy.

I committed to therapy for a solid six weeks, exploring a range of modalities, including the conventional gym sessions, soothing massage, and water therapy. During aquatic therapy, I found myself in the company of a group predominantly comprised of older women. It became apparent that my presence was a welcome diversion to the women. It seemed they found comfort in the pool not just for physical relief but for the social aspect as well. During those sessions, I became a confidante, taking part in a cascade of conversations and gossip. It was an unexpected, and amusing, twist to my therapeutic experience.

Despite the welcomed social interactions, the therapy, while beneficial to some extent, offered only partial relief. My neck persisted to cause discomfort. Because of this, I decided to explore my options and contacted the spine institute at the Cleveland Clinic. Scheduling the appointment with the surgeon, I realized my recovery journey was going to take a new twist.

After meeting with the surgeon a few times and going through another battery of tests, we decided to move forward with the surgery. The surgeon recommended a posterior cervical decompression and fusion. Using this approach, the surgeon opens the back of the neck, removes part of the offending bone, grids up that bone, and replaces it in the space. Over time, the bone graft and the vertebrae fuse together, creating a more solid and stable structure. There is more pain in the healing process when going through the back of the neck, but because of the discs involved, this was deemed the better way to go.

The surgery was scheduled for mid-October. Beth was starting a new job around that time, so our son, Nate, who worked remotely, agreed to come home and help with my recovery. I was very nervous upon arriving at the clinic the morning of the surgery. The procedure would be an all-day affair. After being prepped for surgery, they wheeled me through what seemed to be miles of hallways. Entering the operating arena, there was a team of doctors waiting for me. The last thing I remember is telling the anesthesiologist to not give me too much of that drug.

I have little memory of waking up in my hospital room. Nate and Beth were there, and they tell me I wanted to eat, and I wanted a steak! This was probably ten o'clock at night, and a steak was out of the question. At one point, I asked Nate, "Why did Rapunzel not let down her hair to that guy?"

Laughing, Nate said, "Dad, I don't know the answer to that!" I was so heavily medicated my memory of this does not exist.

I was in the hospital for three days. When I arrived home, I was in extreme pain. Luckily, I had medications to help with the pain. Now, I have never been a person to take drugs. This was the first time in my life I was dependent on them. Nate took very good care of me, and believe me, I really needed his help. In the first month, I tried not to take the pain pills, but when that pain hit me, I was immediately asking Nate for another pill.

The hardest part for me, besides the pain, was the fact I could not drive. After the first month, when I started feeling a bit more mobile, I would beg Beth to ride to the grocery store with her. Of course, she laughed at me as I never wanted to go to any store with her before. I just wanted to get out of the house. Getting in the car, feeling the sun warm my cheeks, and watching all the people hustling into the store gave me some entertainment during this tedious recovery process.

Before my two month visit to the surgeon, I began weaning myself off the drugs. My pain had subsided to a lower intensity, and my neck felt pretty stable. Arriving at the surgeon's office in Cleveland, I could walk in all on my own, and my neck felt like it might survive. After telling my surgeon I had stopped the drugs, he looked shocked and exclaimed, "You are the first patient who stopped taking pain medications this quick. Congratulations!" I smiled, realizing my recovery was now in a new stage—a drug-free one.

Eight years have passed since my surgery. Still, sporadically, my neck still presents challenges to my daily life. I maintain regular check-ins with my surgeon, usually through Zoom, once a year. His stance on my condition is clear: surgical intervention would only be considered if my symptoms escalate to a severe level. It is not lost on me that having to go through a major surgery would be no joke.

As I age, I realize the journey in life is undoubtedly a challenging one, demanding resilience, patience, and a steadfast commitment to taking one day at a time. The road to recovery may be arduous, but with each step forward, we reclaim a sense of control and rediscover our capability to withstand uncomfortable situations. Even though I am not pain-free, surrounding myself with a supportive family allows me to embrace gradual progress. Surviving a back injury is not just about physical healing but also a testament to the indomitable spirit of never giving up and hoping for a better outcome.

Chapter 28 – Southwest Ho!

The dawn of 2019 brought in a plethora of exhilarating and frenzied adventures for my family. In May, my youngest son, Nic, proudly donned his graduation cap, marking the culmination of his college journey. His accomplishment was further magnified by the fact he had already secured a job in the sunny desert in the southwest city of Phoenix, Arizona.

To embark on this cross-country journey, we orchestrated a caravan of three cars to move Nic and his girlfriend, Sunny, to their new home in Tempe, a suburb of Phoenix, Arizona. The caravan kicked off for me in Ohio, where I joined forces with the other participants, rendezvousing in Missouri. Our convoy comprised of Link and me, Nic and Beth, and Sunny, accompanied by her brother. As we charted our course, the caravan proceeded across the country, leaving the Midwest and traveling through the rolling landscapes of Oklahoma, Texas, and New Mexico. Finally, we crossed the threshold into northern Arizona, where the allure of adventure mingled with the anticipation of new beginnings.

Spending the night by Flagstaff, we resumed our journey the next morning. Nic was scheduled to move into his apartment in Tempe in the afternoon. The trip from Flagstaff to Tempe usually takes about two hours, straight down the mountains. We had been on the road heading down the mountain for about 20 minutes when, suddenly, my Tahoe truck began to spew out oil all over the road and the car directly behind me. The motor immediately stopped, and we all pulled over to the side of the road. Jumping out of the truck, I could see oil all over Sunny's car. I shouted, "I think my engine blew up! Is everyone okay?"

Link said, "This is crazy. But I think we all survived!"

"We are all okay, but your truck isn't," Beth added, shaking her head in disbelief.

As we gathered around on the side of the road, I called for a tow truck. We were in the middle of nowhere, so I could only give out a mile marker as our location. Because we were so far away from civilization, we had to wait well over three hours for help to come. Link and I waited along the side of the road as everyone else continued on to Tempe in order to allow Nic to check in at his assigned time. While we waited, a couple of cars stopped to see if we were okay. After what seemed like hours, finally, the tow truck driver arrived.

I was relieved, but that relief soon turned to an uncomfortable dismay. Promptly the taciturn driver loaded up my truck and proceeded on down the mountain. The road was not only steep but very curvy. The driver would not talk to us, and he drove so fast I held onto my seat for dear life. The closest car dealer was in Cottonwood, Arizona, which was at least an hour away from where we had broken down. Finally arriving at the dealership, I immediately got out of the truck and went into the building. "Can I please talk to the owner?" I inquired anxiously of the receptionist.

"Of course. Give me a minute to page him," she replied.

"Hello, can I help you?" a large, gray-haired gentleman said as he held out his hand. Shaking his hand, I explained my concerns about the tow truck driver. "Your driver was very rude. Not only would he not talk to us, he drove like a maniac. I could feel the truck sliding as we went around the curves! He should be fired" I exclaimed.

Frowning, the owner apologized but explained the driver was not his to fire, as they only contracted with the towing company. "Let me get you taken care of," he added.

After getting my truck in the shop, they provided a pickup truck for me to use. Luckily, with the help of the dealership employees, we transferred everything in my truck to the pickup. By this time, it was getting toward evening, and we still had to drive to Tempe which was at least one hour south.

Tired, hungry, and despondent, we arrived in Tempe. As we walked into Nic's apartment, everyone was anxiously wondering about the prognosis of my truck. We did not yet know as the dealership had to examine it and get back with me. The vehicle was only two years old, so it was a mystery to me why the engine had, more or less, blown up. The following day, it was discovered that a gasket had come off, and all the oil had come out of the engine, causing it to seize up.

After numerous phone calls and a series of tense negotiations, a brand new engine was installed in my truck. Thanks to the support of the dealership from which I had originally purchased the vehicle, the entire process unfolded with minimal financial impact on my end. The culmination of this saga transpired over a span of just over two weeks. In the aftermath, I found myself in possession of a brand-new engine in my two year old vehicle. Not only was my son securely settled into his new apartment, but an unexpected silver lining emerged—two weeks of unforeseen vacation for us in the valley of the sun.

Chapter 29 – Finding a Family Home

After our exciting journey moving Nic to Tempe, we went back to Ohio for the summer, with plans to return to the dessert in the fall. Since we intended to leave the frigid winters in Ohio once more, we officially became snowbirds! Early in December, we left Ohio, traversing the same route as earlier in the year. By this time, both our sons had moved to Tempe. Nate had a two-bedroom apartment in the same complex as Nic. To our pleasure, Nate welcomed us into his second bedroom.

The apartment complex was located on Tempe Town Lake, and it had some pretty nice amenities. The apartments, along with the amenities, came with a large price tag—the rent for both apartments was extremely high. We had been there a few weeks, celebrating Christmas with family. Nic came to us in January and said, "I've been researching real estate, and I really don't want to live in this apartment for another year. They have houses out here with casitas—like mother-in-law suites. I think we could live much cheaper if we buy a house." We were immediately intrigued, as we had dabbled in real estate over the years. Using our combined incomes, we contacted a banker and got pre-approved for a mortgage loan.

Through searching on the internet, we found a couple of houses on the west side of the valley that we wanted to look at. Nic had been working with a realtor in

Scottsdale, but he contacted the realtor who was named on the listing of the one house we had found. Touring both houses turned out to be a major disappointment, as they both were not to our liking. Immediately, Beth started searching on her phone for other properties and just happened to find a house close by that had just listed. Luckily, the realtor contacted the listing agent and said we could get in that day. Driving up to the house, we were unimpressed with the looks, but walking in, we all were very impressed with the interior. The house was fairly new, very large, freshly painted, and had all the amenities we were looking for, proving that exterior looks can be deceiving.

We made an offer about ten percent lower than the asking price. In no time, the sellers turned down our offer. Disappointed, we decided to wait and keep looking. Thirty days passed, and we did not hear anything from the realtor. We kept an eye on the house we were interested in. One day, I found the price had dropped by $10,000. Not hearing anything from the realtor, I contacted her, and she was not aware of the price drop. I was incensed by the fact this realtor was not doing her job. We knew more than her!

Considering the lack of knowledge this realtor had, Nic contacted his original realtor in Scottsdale and asked if he would write up an offer on the house. Even though that realtor dealt mostly with east valley real estate, he agreed to write up an offer. Surprisingly, the sellers immediately accepted our offer. We were ecstatic with the prospect of becoming homeowners in Arizona. As we eagerly awaited closing, the original realtor contacted Nic's realtor, claiming to have some rights to the commission. We had not signed any paperwork with her, so her attempt to intimidate fell through. We all apologized to our realtor and explained to him what had transpired. He understood our position and told us not to worry about the threat.

At last, without further complications, our loan was finalized. This marked the onset of the pandemic, during which most businesses were closing down. Undeterred by the challenging circumstances, we planned our relocation toward the end of May. The moving team came and efficiently packed up our belongings from two separate apartments, transporting them all across the valley to deliver into our new house. Despite the exhaustive process that took most of the day, the satisfaction of seeing our furniture and clothes in their designated places brought a collective sigh of relief. Contently, we laid our heads down to rest, grateful to have successfully moved during such a difficult time.

Speaking of difficult, four days later, Beth and Nic both became ill. This was so early on in the pandemic there was no quick way to test for Covid. Nic was mildly sick for a few days, but Beth's symptoms lingered. She was extremely tired and wanted to sleep the days away. Finally, I literally dragged her to urgent care. They tested her for Covid but could not tell her if she was infected. By the time she received the positive results, ten days later, she had recovered and was healthy again. The strange part of this disease was I never contracted the virus, yet I was around her and Nic the entire time. This illustrates the weirdness of Covid, like how some people get it while others seem to be immune. Luckily, none of us were affected long-term by the virus.

After recovering from the virus, it was time for our return journey to Ohio. An unexpected silver lining of the pandemic was the unusually sparse traffic, which made our trip more comfortable. Reassured by the fact we had a home to return to in the upcoming fall, we embarked on our journey.

In the subsequent months following our purchase, the real estate market in the Phoenix area experienced a remarkable and dramatic surge. Our initial purchase, once a simple transaction to save on high rent, swiftly transformed into a shrewd investment as the value of our house soared. Recognizing this opportunity, we decided to enhance our property by adding a pool and landscaping in the backyard. This served as a perfect heartfelt Christmas gift to our sons. How's that for killing two birds with one stone?

Chapter 30 – Snow Birds

Now that we were officially snow birds, we began our Arizona experience by joining the local recreation center. The events offered by the recreation center for seniors included monthly bingo, a dice game called bunco, and various card games. We enjoyed these events immensely, as they not only offered entertainment but allowed us to meet other senior members of the community. Every so often, the center also offered day trips to various sites around Arizona.

One day trip stands out in my mind, as we traveled to Apache Junction, Arizona, for Barleens Rockin' and Rollin' Lunch Show. Barleens is a staple in Apache Junction, as they have provided entertainment for many years. Walking into the facility, we were amazed by the vastness of the dinner theater. Our favorite part of the lunch was having the decadent dessert first; Barleens says, "Life is short. Eat dessert first!" Of course, this is right up my alley, as my sweet tooth is always active and encouraging me to indulge. The show, of course, was immensely entertaining and had us all laughing at the crazy humor and humming along to the songs.

Influenced by my mother's love for watching old westerns on our black and white TV, I dreamed of visiting an old western cowboy town. Approximately three hours south of where we stayed is the historic western town of Tombstone. We decided to plan a day trip to visit this historic site. Tombstone, nestled in the rugged terrain of southeastern Arizona, emerges as a living testament to the bygone era of the Wild, Wild West. It is a historic town, with dusty streets and well-preserved buildings, which allows visitors to step back in time and relive the legendary tales which my mother and I watched many times on our old TV.

Early one morning, while traveling with Beth and her sister and brother-in-law, we headed south for the old mining town. I felt great anticipation about finally getting to experience this western town which had long-ago attracted a colorful cast of characters, from prospectors seeking fortune in the mines to the notorious outlaws seeking refuge from the law. I had visions in my head of Doc Holliday and Wyatt Earp and the O.K. Corral gun fight.

Arriving in Tombstone, my initial impression was one of dismay. The town appeared to be a cheap replica of the vision I had in my head. Walking out of the parking lot, we headed for the main street, where we saw the Bird Cage Theatre, with its weathered façade, rising up to welcome us. Various cowboys and glamorous courtesans sauntered by, inviting us into the lively establishments. Strolling down the boardwalk, we decided to eat lunch before attending the infamous reenactment at the O.K. Corral.

After our enjoyable lunch, my initial dismay turned to amazement as we began the journey back in time. The preserved history, forever etched in Western lore, made Tombstone a realistic voyage into the Old West. The sun cast long shadows over us as we strolled through the streets, absorbing the sights and sounds of the town. The O.K. Corral reenactment allowed us to imagine the tension that once gripped the people of the town on that fateful day. We especially enjoyed reading about the lives and struggles of the cast of characters who lived in Tombstone. My fascination with the old west was fully satisfied as I learned about and observed how Big Nose Kate, Doc Holliday, and the Earps all lived and survived during those days. I had a smile on my face as we left Tombstone to head back to our neck of the woods, leaving the Old West far behind.

With my dream fulfilled, other activities took precedence. I never realized that Beth and I had so many relations in the Phoenix area. On Beth's side of the family, there were nine great nieces and/or nephews, and most of them played some type of sport. On my side of the family, there were about five cousins of a young age. Oftentimes, we would travel to their games, which included football, baseball, softball, soccer, volleyball, and even hockey.

The desert climate provided an ideal setting for year-round outdoor sports, and as a result, a significant portion of our time in Arizona was spent following and enjoying athletic endeavors. The younger boys, in particular, would light up with joy upon spotting me at their various events. The air would resonate with exuberant voices calling out, "Hi, Uncle Chester!" Given that I was often the sole person of color in the park, it inevitably attracted attention from the predominately white crowd, turning heads in curiosity. Surprisingly, though I was a bit embarrassed, I never felt uncomfortable, as the genuine excitement of the kids overshadowed any of the external factors.

Another amusing incident occurred at a local coffee shop, where we gathered with Beth's niece and her four children. Seated around the table, we engaged in lively conversation, enjoyed our meals, and savored some truly excellent coffee. Unexpectedly, I felt a sensation on my arm, initially mistaking it for a bug. Upon closer inspection, I discovered the youngest great-niece's fingers delicately exploring my brown skin. Startled when our eyes met, she jumped slightly. With a chuckle, I reassured her, saying, "It's brown—it won't come off!" She blushed and withdrew her hand, and we all shared a hearty laugh. I empathized with her curiosity, realizing that she hadn't been exposed to very much diversity in her upbringing.

From the time I first met Beth's family, they embraced me wholeheartedly; extending the warm acceptance and kinship of family. The amazing fact was this acceptance was not just limited to the immediate family but was passed down through generations. Their children and grandchildren mirrored the same inclusive attitude. I treat all of my young nieces, nephews, and cousins the same, regardless of which side of the family they come from. Reflecting on these experiences, one can't help but envision a world free from prejudice if only everyone could emulate such kindness and unity.

Chapter 31- Reflections

While writing this transcript, I found myself reflecting on all that has transpired over the course of my life. Writing about my childhood challenges, my youthful vigor, and my immediate and extended family has allowed me to further understand just how durable I have been over the course of 70-plus years. Even with my failings, I have found solace in realizing it is never too late to learn—my life has been a long journey. They say wisdom comes with age, and I've come to wholeheartedly agree. It took me many years to slow down and embrace the art of writing. Perhaps I should have heeded my wife's advice years ago!

Throughout my life, I've held onto core values that sustain me: keeping God in my life, helping people, showing respect, and supporting my family. While this transcript only scratches the surface of the entirety of my life experiences, it underscores the resilience of the human spirit. I've learned that our beginnings don't define us; it's the choices we make along the way that shape our journey. I am far from perfect, but I own up to and acknowledge my shortcomings and constantly strive to improve and grow.

In the tapestry of life, resilience weaves its intricate threads, forming a pattern of strength and fortitude amidst the trials we face. Like a master weaver, resilience stitches together the fabric of our existence, reinforcing our ability to overcome adversity and flourish in the face of challenges. Happily, I look forward to the remaining years with my wife and family, enjoying the daily experience, until God calls me home.

www.ingramcontent.com/pod-product-compliance
Lightning Source LLC
Chambersburg PA
CBHW071117160426
43196CB00013B/2609